Lydia and Joachim F. Richter

Collecting Antique Dolls

Fashion Dolls • Automata • Doll Curiosities • Exclusive Dolls

A special section contains tips on collecting dolls by Carolyn Cook, Managing Editor of Doll Reader® magazine.

Doll Reader® — *The Ultimate Authority*

Published by Hobby House Press Cumberland Maryland 21502

Acknowledgments

Publisher: Hobby House Press, Inc.

Concept and layout: Joachim F. Richter

Text: Lydia Richter, Antoon van Aken, Ann-Marie Porot

Title of Original Edition: "Puppen Raritäten," by Verlag Laterna Magica Joachim F. Richter, Munich, Germany

Photographs: Alfred Barsotti: pages 4 (below left), 6-9, 16-19, 20 below, 24, 25, 28-31, 34, 36, 37, 39 below, 40-52, 64, 65, 90-93, 96-100, 102, 103; Jean-Marc Breguet: 26, 27; Kath Engels: 20 above; Ella Hass: 88 left above; Studio Kleiber: 63; Legoland: 68 below right, 88 middle; Carin Lossnitzer: 53, 108 above; "Musée d'art et d'histoire" Neuchatel: 26, 27; Joachim F. Richter: 15, 20 above left, 23, 32 left above, 33, 38, 39 above, 54, 66, 68, 72, 73, 95, 104, 105; Lydia Richter: 66, 67, 69, 86, 94, 101, 106-109; Hannelore Schenkelberger: cover, 5, 54, 55, 57, 59, 62, 70, 71, 74-85; Karin Schmelcher: 4 above, 32 below, 89; Stadtmuseum Munich: 35; Museum Stein am Rhein: 21, 22.

The authors and publisher would like to thank those who furnished photographs and loaned dolls for this book: Alfred Barsotti, Mrs. Gau, Mrs. Gauder-Bonnet, Ella Hass, Dr. Höllesberger, Carin Lossnitzer, Hannelore Schenkelberger, Karin Schmelcher, Mrs. Stix, Doll Collection from the Museum of the City of Munich, Doll Museum Katharina Engels, Rothenburg o. T., Doll Museum, Stein am Rhein, Doll Museum Legoland and the Doll Department of the Museum in Neuchatel.

Sources: *Dolls* Max von Boehm

Translation: Michael T. Robertson

Published by Cumberland, Maryland 21502

Hobby House Press

ISBN: 0-87588-362-1

Table of Contents

Introduction

Lovers and collectors of old dolls have always existed, but since old dolls have started to be viewed as real antiques, doll collecting has become a recognized and fascinating hobby worldwide. Thus, the interest in information about the dolls and their producers has grown, as well as the need for excellent colored photographs, which can help in identification as well as show the beauty of these dolls.

A very rare 21½in (55cm) Steiner "D," of which only three examples are supposedly still in existence in Europe.

The author began compiling information about dolls some time ago. Much has already been unearthed, some will still be discovered and other information will remain a secret. Some of the most important data can be found in old catalogs and leaflets. For example, original clothing can be identified and the doll's date of production can be determined. However, it is very difficult and in some cases, nearly impossible to locate old documents dating prior to 1900. Features of the dolls are sometimes unrecognizable because either the photograph is too small or there is only a hand-drawn sketch. Therefore, frequently reprints or originals of old catalogs do not offer enough criteria the collector of today requires.

Fortunately, there are still a large number of old dolls available and even though they cannot speak, they are still able tell us a lot about themselves. For example, the marking on the back of the neck or on the breastplate gives important information about the producer. Should the marking not be available, since dolls were seldom completely marked before 1890, then certain features on the head or body can convey information.

Up until ten years ago, French dolls with closed mouths were considered to be the most desirable antique dolls, but now many of the top German models are also included. Dolls from France were always famous worldwide — especially known for their luxurious clothing. Dolls from Bru, Jumeau, Steiner and Gaultier have always enraptured collectors, whether it was play, automata or fashion dolls. Now the interest has turned more and more towards the German dolls, of which there are a large number of different types. In the last few years the very expressive character dolls have found great attention. Many beautiful German dolls, however, which were produced between 1870 and 1890, have attracted little attention.

Fashion doll from Gaultier with a bisque head.

This book acts as a guide, drawing attention to the most beautiful earlier dolls with molded hair and towards several unusual Kestner dolls (such as the Kestner A.T.-type, page 75).

For the present, let us say a few more words about the original German title, *Doll Rarities*. Beginning with the fact that today old dolls and toys should be generally considered as being rare, we would like to point out, however, that in this book only special and extraordinary doll rarities are presented, those which very few get to see. Even at doll fairs or antique markets they have become rather rare. The word "rarity" used in conjunction with this book and its original title not only applies to the rare dolls or automata, but also applies to the exquisite original clothing, to unusual groups like the small nuns (see pages 104 and 105), and to the small orchestra with their musical instruments (page 103). In this case, the rarity lies not only with the individual dolls, but to the whole group with their instruments. This word "rarity" is widely used in this book; it includes everything that is unusual — outstanding beauty, rareness, amusing and curios.

Thus, we are very pleased to introduce to you these small treasures in full color and we would like to thank all those doll friends who have contributed towards this book with photographic material, especially Hannelore Schenkelberger and Alfred Barsotti, as well as several doll museums.

An early 19¼in (49cm) Kestner; light bisque, dark blue glass sleep eyes, mohair wig on plaster dome, composition body with ten joints; circa 1890.

5

French Fashion Dolls

In the middle of the 19th century, the first fashion dolls with porcelain heads were created in France. Several exceptional examples are introduced herein.

These fashion dolls were created in a period when they were supposed to present the latest Parisian fashions to the world, but at the same time were freed from this duty, because suddenly modern printing methods made the distribution of printed fashion engravings and fashion magazines possible. The magazines could also include patterns, making it possible for dressmakers to produce these dresses. Now that they were unemployed, the extraordinary popularity of these fashion dolls did not change. They were now solely produced, sold, loved and collected for their beauty and elegance. At the same time, they advanced more and more to a play doll for young growing-up girls, because the fashion doll was always and still is a charming and diversified toy, if possible with a trousseau full of dresses and accessories, which also had a certain educational meaning.

Girls of that period learned how to dress properly; also, they took great pleasure in learning how to sew so that they could make all the small accessories which would make their little loved ones look beautiful. For this purpose a commercial magazine including patterns was printed in France. It was called *La Poupée Modèle* in France and *Puppenmütterchens Nähstube* (Doll-mothers Sewing-room) in Germany. Due to the fact that girls at that time were being prepared for the most important role in their lives as a wife and mother, many manufacturers were increasingly producing bride-to-be dolls. These found great popularity for a long time. (See page 19.)

Fashion doll from Huret with trousseau, bisque head, body made from metal; markings found on back: "HURET 68 RUE de la BOETIE;" circa 1865.

The Meaning of Fashion and Dolls

To understand the meaning of fashion dolls, it should be pointed out how important fashion was back in the last centuries. Today, one cannot comprehend this because today's fashion recommends certain designs, materials and colors, but it is left to the individual, whether to conform or not. One can wear whatever one likes without attracting notice. It does not make a difference today, whether the skirt is somewhat longer or shorter, or that the waistline is worn higher or lower. Everything is allowed; the more leisurely and practical, the better. Thank God! Corsets, which were absolute torture-tools and rather damaging for one's health, have disappeared. However, it was not too long ago that fashion changed as its dictates were still strongly felt at the beginning of the 20th century. Those who did not submit could have lost their reputations quite easily. Thus it was common that some families preferred to forgo a good meal rather than fashionable clothing. Yet we have to view the past fashion with different aspects.

Not too long ago a young girl could only see her future in a marriage. Therefore, to make a good match, she was forced to use her bodily charm and to do this she needed very lovely and expensive clothing. Low-cut dresses, wasp waists and wide-swinging skirts were all supposed to arouse men and encourage them to marry. Therefore, the fashion doll had the very important task of showing these lovely dresses, naturally according to the latest fashion, to the rest of the world. However, today all this is not necessary. Young girls can choose their own jobs and decide their own lives.

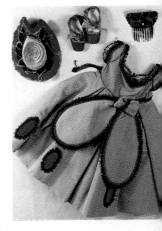

One of the dresses from the trousseau belonging to the Huret doll on the opposite page.

Historical

The history of the fashion doll can be retraced from today right back to about 1300. The person who first decided to dress a doll with the appropriate clothing and use it as a model on his journeys remains unknown and will no doubt remain so. We do know that French crusaders brought these dolls back from the Orient, showing how the Oriental population dressed. Therefore, the idea that these dolls may have been the inspiration for the fashion doll may not be so far wrong.

In any case, France is referred to as the country of origin for the fashion doll, which is made credible, since Parisian fashion has always had a major worldwide role.

The first historical and authentic information concerning fashion dolls, or mannequins as they would be called today, has been found in written reports, bills and naturally in paintings and the first historical evidence of a fashion mannequin comes from the year 1396, according to existing information. Queen Isabelle of France had ordered one to be made and dressed luxuriously. It was then sent to the Queen of England so that she could be kept

Dress with black lace trimmings from the trousseau belonging to the Huret doll on page 6.

informed about the latest Parisian fashions. This incident is documented with an invoice from the court tailor, Robert de Varemes, for the sum of 459 francs, which at that time was a very large amount, so that one is lead to believe that the mannequin must have had the size of a normal person and wore the original sized clothing.

In the following centuries, further information comes down about fashion dolls from which one can deduce, that at first individual dolls, often given as gifts, presented the latest fashion at the courts. Only in the 17th century did the fashion doll find her way into the lower circle of nobility and later into the middle class. Furetière reports that the fiction writer Mlle de Scudery owned two fashion dolls (which were named at that time Pandora) and that the larger one wore an evening dress and that the smaller one a negligee. These dolls were at first sent to England from France and later on to many other ruling countries.

This arrangement did not only elicit enthusiasm, but also ridicule and disapproval. For example, in 1689 an anonymous satire complained: "And this is the worst possible thing that could happen, not only do the women travel to France themselves, but they also let themselves be sent models, dressed up dolls, for a lot of money, so that they could copy by all means the latest court fashions." This was most likely written by a husband who had to foot the high bills. This did not help very much, since the triumphant progression of the fashion doll was not to be held up. An English newspaper had announced in 1712 that in a house on King Street, Covent Garden, a French doll had just arrived. From this doll, the dressmakers copied the fashion for the whole year, until the next doll arrived in the following year. In 1723, these beautiful and luxuriously dressed dolls from France were already mentioned in a trade book, so that one can conclude that these dolls were not sent individually anymore, but that an organized company was involved. Right up until 1850, the fashion doll experienced its golden age, until, as mentioned at the beginning, it had lost its significance in the fashion world due to fashion journals and prints.

Appearance and Materials of Fashion Dolls

The fashion doll is quickly recognized by its appearance, because it does not resemble a doll with childlike features, but only that of a fashionably dressed young lady. As such, her body has the proportions of a grown-up. A relatively small head is attached to a longish body with a slim waist. This mannequin figure was an important feature for the wearing of elegant clothing. This extravagant fashionable clothing was and is the most important thing about a fashion doll and is often more valuable than the doll itself.

In old prints and paintings one can find fashion dolls from the early period, but none of these old samples has survived the past centuries. One can only imagine the types of materials of which they were made. It can only be assumed that most of them were carved from wood because it was easier to work with and due to its durability and consistency, it could survive the very long journeys.

During the last century, many different kinds of materials were used to produce fashion dolls. That most commonly used for the head was wood, wax, papier-mâché (also with a wax coating), gutta-percha and from approximately 1850 onwards, porcelain and from about 1860 to 1870, bisque. The hairdos were carved into the wood, painted on, molded on, but also fur or real hair was glued on, until around 1870 on, when wigs started to dominate. At first the porcelain head consisted of a head, neck and breast made from one piece (a so-called breastplate head), but already from 1861 on, the more exclusive dolls had their heads separately mounted onto a shoulder plate (both were made from porcelain), so that the head could be turned (a socket breast head).

A very unusual two-piece dress of the Huret doll on page 6.

For the production of the bodies one used wood, gutta-percha, metal, composition, cloth and mainly leather. The dolls could be made completely out of one kind of material, for example wood or gutta-percha, but most of the time they were combined with different materials, such as wood, wax or papier-mâché, or porcelain heads were mostly attached to leather bodies. The forearms and hands were made at first from leather, but later out of porcelain.

The very lovely clothing was made at first by hand from materials of that period, mainly cotton, silk, velvet, wool, plush and others. Only as the sewing machine was invented around 1850, did one start to use it to sew the longer seams. However, many of the smaller seams and hems, as well as the richly decorative embroidery and trimmings were still done by hand. Jumeau mentions in an advertisement from 1870 various materials — wool muslin, plush, serge, piqué, stuff, cashmere, cheviot, batiste and pyrenaen wool.

The outfitting of these dolls, starting with the night and undergarments, which were richly trimmed with lace, did not end, however, with the clothing alone. There were also beautifully decorated hats with feathers and flowers, as well as shoes. They were also completely equipped with accessories which a lady in real life would need such as handbags, parasols, umbrellas, gloves, handkerchiefs, corsets, combs, hairbrushes, mirrors and other items. All this put together made up a large trousseau, which also contained several other dresses for changing into.

Very soon a complete supply industry was involved in the manufacture of the actual doll, which settled down around the Passage Choiseu in Paris: dolls' shoe and hat makers, as well as glove, corset and wig makers. At that time the hard working manufacturers knew how to increase their sales. The accessories for the dolls were placed into doll suitcases and were sold together with the doll. Also included was a letter of advice, offering doll mothers help concerning when and how to change their doll children's dresses, make new hairdos or when they should be dressed in new clothes.

Now we come to the individual important French fashion doll producers.

Huret, Paris

One of the first significant fashion doll producers of the 19th century was Mlle. Adelaide Calixte Huret. She succeeded with the help of her father in constructing a jointed doll made out of gutta-percha, which, in 1855, won a silver medal at an international exhibition. The dressing table for this doll was also well praised, the remark being made that it had been well made and that it was also of good taste. After this success, Mlle. Huret was permitted to imprint onto the leather band of the doll, which joined the gutta-percha body and the porcelain shoulder head, the following inscription: "Maison Montmatre Paris," and in addition, the picture of Napoleon III with the comment: "EXPOSITION UNIVERSELLE 1855." Unfortunately, gutta-percha was not very durable and therefore, it is rather difficult to find such a doll in good condition today.

HURET

[Body marking of a Huret]

From 1860 on Mlle. Huret produced her doll heads in her own porcelain factory located in L'Isle-Adam near Paris. They were made in one piece and consisted of glazed porcelain or bisque. The eyes were painted, mainly blue, the eyelids were formed relief-like, and the mouth was well defined, closed and painted red. Quite often one will find a wig glued to the head made of sheep's or Tibet goats' hair. The neck is short and the shoulders are rounded, just like most of the dolls of that period. The body is long-limbed, has joints and soft forms.

Her gutta-percha dolls were produced until approximately 1880. However, it is possible to find doll bodies made of wood with similar joints and with the same markings. All of these bodies were very well made and later one will find bodies made of metal or leather with hands made of lead. In 1867 Mlle. Huret once again took part in an international exhibition in Paris and again won a silver medal. Isabelle Charlier, who made the clothing for her, received a "Honorable Mention" because the clothing was elegant and was in very good taste.

As a rule, the clothing, like the body of the doll, was marked: "Huret." From 1867 on, all Huret dolls were marked on the breast with the new mark of distinction: "MEDAILLE D'ARGENT" and "EXPOSITION UNIVERSELLE 1867." From 1865 on, one will find the name Huret combined with Longchambon in the annual trade books, whereas from 1869 on, only the name of her successor, Longchambon, with the address "Boulevard Montmatre 22" appears. The reputation of the Huret company was so good that the successor continued to use this name. That is why one will still find the name Huret in a lot of advertisements from 1930.

Rohmer, Paris

Around 1860 Mlle. Huret received competition from Mlle. Lèontine Rohmer, who used the patent of her brother-in-law, Reidmeister, to produce doll bodies made out of punched-out metal, and sold fashion dolls, which were very similar to those of Huret. Mlle. Huret, who was very proud of her dolls and was afraid of business losses, did not like this at all and thus made an appeal. Mlle. Rohmer and her brother-in-law, Reidmeister, had to make way and around 1880, suspended their production. In spite of all this, these dolls are very valuable collectors' pieces today, as are those of Mlle. Huret.

Gaultier, Paris

One name should not be missing at all in connection with fashion dolls: Francois Gaultier (not Fernand, which up until not long ago was still taken for granted). In 1860, he founded his own porcelain factory, specializing in the production of painted porcelain doll heads and parts of excellent quality, for which he won a

F 5 G

[Neck marking of a Gaultier]

11

silver medal. For that period he was one of the most important producers of doll heads and due to his high standard of quality, was able to acquire a very large clientele. However, he did not produce any doll bodies and that explains why one will find his doll heads on doll bodies made by other French manufacturers, such as Bru, Jumeau, Gesland and others.

The first heads of Gaultier were unmarked. From 1870 on, they were marked with "F.G." or "F.G." and a number, or later with a border. In 1880, as Gaultier retired from business, his two eldest sons took over. To begin with, they won silver medals at large international exhibitions: 1883 in Amsterdam, 1884 in Nizza, 1885 in Antwerp and 1889 in Paris. At the end of the 19th century, the brothers had to compete with the French and the foreign manufacturers. In 1899, they decided (under compulsion) to unite with the joint venture group S.F.B.J. One thing is certain. The products of the sons never did reach the quality of those of the father.

Bru, Paris

Leon Casimir Bru, who started manufacturing dolls in 1867, also produced at first fashion dolls, even though in smaller volume. That is why today they are especially rare and coveted collectors' pieces. Bru most likely obtained his doll heads from Gaultier. The peculiarity of these lovely ladies' faces was that they had a light feigned smile around the corners of the mouth, which is why they are today known by as the *Mona Lisas* or *Smiling Brus*. The bodies were made of leather, wood and gutta-percha.

Jumeau, Paris

Pierre Francois Jumeau and M. Belton founded their doll maker's shop in Paris in 1842 and started out at first producing fashion dolls. In that same year an advertisement in the *Annual Trade Book* listed "Belton and Jumeau, Producers of Fashion Dolls, Dolls made of Leather and clothed." That meant that these dolls had leather bodies and not only presented the latest fashion, but served also as toys. It is a great pity that the material used for the head was never mentioned. However, since the doll industry had no porcelain heads around 1842, it is assumed that they were either made of wood, wax or papier-mâché. It is very difficult to verify this since the Jumeau doll heads from that period were all unmarked.

JUMEAU,
MEDAILLE D'OR
PARIS

[Body marking of a doll from Emile Jumeau; circa 1870]

In 1844, Jumeau and Belton presented dolls at an exhibition in Paris and received a bronze medal, as well as an order from the Ministry of Trade for dressed dolls so that the French fashion could also be presented in China. One has learned from the stories told by the jury that the manufacture of the clothing was very well done, that the company's trading was growing steadily and that they were exporting.

In 1846, Pierre Francois Jumeau separated from Belton and continued his successful career by himself. Once again he received a bronze medal at the National Exhibition of Industry in Paris. Finally, in 1849, Natalie Rondot reports: "The leather doll is produced in Paris with such beautiful work, good taste and of good value, that they are exported to all countries of this world. They find and fear no other competition. These facts, through the Exhibition of Monsieur Jumeau, establish a special kind of interest: his sales lie around 120.000 Francs, that most of his products are exported and are well known as far as China."

In 1855, Jumeau received a silver medal at the World's Fair in Paris for his elegant style and good taste, for which the products of his company were always distinguished. It is also mentioned that he not only produced luxury dolls, but also rather simple dolls — with and without a trousseau — which were all carefully dressed and whose prices explained the large sales in France as well as abroad. Not until after 1860 did Jumeau advertise his dolls with porcelain heads. However, one can assume that he obtained these from the Gaultier porcelain factory, as well as from Germany, because he only started producing his own heads in 1873, when he opened up a porcelain factory in Montreuil-sous-Bois.

One can surely say that Jumeau, until this point in time, owed his prizes and medals more to his exceptionally beautiful doll clothes than to the dolls themselves, the latter not receiving a word of praise until then. It is known that he used all of his love and talent for fashion and because of his exquisite taste for elegant clothing, established a worldwide reputation for his dolls.

For the production of the lovely clothing for his dolls and the trousseau, he employed home workers for many years, until around 1880, when he opened up his own shop. In an advertisement from 1879, he listed his clothed or unclothed dolls, with or without trousseaus, in various different models. Here is an example of a suitcase which contained the following items: "A shirt for the day, a shirt for the night, a pair of lace-trimmed breeches and a lace-trimmed undergarment, a corset made of satin, a bonnet made of silk richly decorated with lace, a pair of stockings and a pair of cream colored shoes, a dress made of pique richly decorated with embroidery, a coat lined with wadding and braided edging."

[Neck marking of a doll from Emile Jumeau; circa 1870]

Particularly worth mentioning are his wonderful models of brides, one which is shown on pages 18 and 19.

In 1878, Jumeau (or rather his son, Emile) received a gold medal. This time it was not only for the clothing, but also for the wonderful doll. At this time, fashion dolls were also being pushed into the background here by the bébé.

The End of the Fashion Doll

Around 1880, the interest in fashion dolls was slowly coming to an end. Although they were very much liked as toys, the ladies among the dolls were surpassed by the childlike bébé. Fashion dolls were now only being made in smaller quantities, especially by Bru and Jumeau, who began using them for their original purpose as fashion mannequins. Jumeau especially seemed to still produce a lot of fashion dolls. Thus, in 1897, a report about him appeared in *Pearson's Magazine*, wherein it stated that the lady dolls, which were being produced, were exported to England, Spain and Germany, in order to help the sales of the Parisian fashions in large department stores. Sometimes orders for individual dolls were made, which were then presented to foreign dignitaries as a present or were sold. Reportedly, Jumeau produced a doll with 25 trunks full of clothing and accessories which was delivered to Russia. Unfortunately, this collection has disappeared.

In 1910, one of the most well-known Parisian couturiers, Paul Poiret, tried to bring back the popularity of the fashion doll. He presented his models carrying wonderfully dressed dolls. Soon the public was traveling to Paris to buy the dresses as well as the doll. The dolls were dressed by Madame Paquin and Madame Lanvin, two of the best milliners of Paris.

Did German Fashion Dolls Exist?

Fashion dolls which traveled around the world showing off the latest fashion were not popular in Germany. However, fashionably dressed dolls with ladylike appearances were produced. As a rule, the factory-made clothing was not of high quality. The German manufacturers preferred not to compete with the French and mainly sold their dolls with or without clothing. However, if one happens to find a doll with an extravagantly elegant old wardrobe from Germany, one can be sure that the clothing was made later privately. These dolls, with the ladylike appearances and elegantly dressed, are called German fashion dolls by collector's today so as to distinguish them from the French ones.

7½in (19cm) Biedermeier doll (china head), wooden body, porcelain forearms and legs, painted hair and eyes; circa 1860.

Furthermore, there is another confusing fact that one finds over and over again: German doll heads on French bodies and German dolls with French clothing (see page 64). The explanation for this is that before 1900, many doll heads and completely undressed dolls were exported to France. This is seen from the following study which was made for the occasion of the World's Fair in Paris in 1878: "Our porcelain painters refuse to paint doll heads and therefore our manufacturers are forced to buy in Sonneberg, Coburg or Nürnberg..."

From 1870 on until about the turn of the century, especially beautiful ladylike dolls were produced by companies such as Simon & Halbig, Kestner and C. F. Kling. Kestner's *Gibson Girl*, created around 1900 for export to America, is one of the last in the series of these wonderful and charming ladies.

Round dance of various different dolls.

A very rare 17⅜in (44cm) fashion doll, presumably from
Leon Casimir Bru; socket head (see right page) made of
a fine light bisque on a breastplate, fixed blue glass
eyes, closed mouth, real hair wig, blue-turquoise satin
dress, kid leather body over a wooden frame (very
rare), forearms of bisque, feet of wood; label on
breast; circa 1875.

A LA PETITE AMAZONE
ε 53
BOULEVARD DES ITALIENS
PARIS

Label on the breast.

A beautiful 21⅝in (55cm) bride doll from Jumeau, Paris; socket head made of fine bisque, light blue fixed paperweight eyes, pierced ears, closed mouth, blonde original wig, kid leather body, original clothing; marked: "A.H.;" circa 1875. Bride's dress made of a beige-colored cotton satin, trimmings of Valenciennes lace, bands, pearls, ornamental flowers, flowers made of wax, train made of artistically embroidered tulle. The doll wears leather gloves and in her right hand she is holding a picture Bible and in the left a bunch of flowers.

On top of the hair is a bridal headpiece made of wax flowers, pearls and lace. The undergarments are trimmed with lace, embroidered stockings and white leather gloves.

Above: Rohmer (presumably) unmarked fashion doll made of glazed porcelain.

Right: 18⅞in (48cm) Huret; socket head made of bisque, very complicated wooden body with 11 joints, including the joint at the waist; circa 1870.

A well-shaped wooden body of a Huret fashion doll with ten joints.

Opposite page: Huret; two very rare fashion dolls with bisque heads, clothing in the fashion of that period; circa 1870.

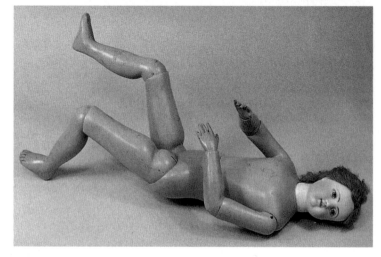

Left page: Rohmer; two very elegant *Pandoras*. Right doll: glazed porcelain head, body and hands made of leather. Left: head and forearms made of bisque, leather body, very beautiful old clothing; circa 1875.

Above: Gaultier; unmarked, socket breast head of bisque, fixed blue eyes, closed mouth, mohair wig, leather body, arms and hands, old clothing made of blue silk, matching umbrella, handbag and gloves; circa 1870.

F. 1 G.

[Neck marking from a Gaultier doll]

15¾in (40cm) Gaultier; fashion doll with breastplate head made of bisque, a very lovely old dress made from gold-colored satin trimmed with wine-red satin, matching hat, decorated with flowers and bows; circa 1870.

Above left: A doll wearing richly decorated lace undergarments. Below: A very unusual and rare body, breastplate head and a wooden body connected to a leather upper part, six joints.

Right-hand page: 14½in (37cm) Gaultier, pleasant fashion doll; socket breast head of bisque, leather body; circa 1875.

Doll Automata

A musician and an artist: Two famous doll automata from the period between 1768 and 1774, made by Jaquet Droz, found at the Historical Museum of Neuchatel.

Past and present, young or old, everyone was and still is delighted by the amusing performance of the doll automata. However, some teachers maintain that mechanical toys are not suitable for children because they give the childlike fantasy no room for imagination. A child should not be allowed to get a mechanical doll into its hands, nor undress it or play with it, because the complicated built-in mechanism could be easily damaged. These arguments are pretty accurate. However, one should point out that every minute the doll automata is allowed to show its funny and graceful antics is a moment of happiness, which can only be justified by the existence of these wonderful toys. Who would like to prove otherwise, that these moments of joy are not capable of hastening a child's fantasy. One should observe a child trying to copy the jerky movements or dances, how they listen totally engrossed to the music coming from such automata, to see how impressed they are.

Although the automata had their height of success in the 19th century, one can follow their story all the way back into the Middle Ages. For example, there is the priest who used biblical figures that could produce all kinds of movements to clearly impress upon his congregation. The first clockwork mechanism was created in the Middle Ages, which later on became very important in the development of doll automata. This technology reached a high standard of perfection especially in Switzerland. Clockwork games were developed with complete scenes with many moving figures. A very good example of this is the town carillon erected in 1530 in Bern, which shows among other things a parade of music-making bears and a crowing, wing beating rooster. Common to all these earlier clocks was the fact that they moved due to heavy lead weights. It is amazing how simple the constructions were at the beginning and how fast they developed into complicated mechanisms capable of producing the most delicate movements. Doll lovers were soon attracted by these technical wonders. Neither cost nor trouble were spared to be able to be surrounded by such ingenious toys. For many an engineer of this period, the designing and building of such automata meant a considerable second income for himself, so that he was capable of financing his own scientific research. As trade in Western Europe was experiencing a great boom in the 17th century, a lot of money was being spent on these movable figures. Famous were the designs made by the Italian physicist Gianelle della Torre, who among other things developed a loud playing lady doll which could walk and move its head and left arm. Many of the French doll manufacturers who were specializing in automata at the end of the 19th century were still being inspired by this example. During the course of the 18th century, exhibitors were beginning to take interest in these automata. Quite often they spent many years of their lives trying to develop one single product, which they then used when visiting the large cities where they could show their machines to the people for a small fee. Even though most of these automata have either been lost or destroyed, those remaining show clearly how refined and with what patience they were created. The most famous of these are the three dolls produced by the Swiss family, Jaquet Droz, a team of father and son. These dolls are currently located at the Historical Museum of Neuchâtel. One of these dolls writes, the other draws and the third, a young lady, plays a piano. Of all three, the doll which can write is a technical wonder. This boy can write passages with up to 40 characters on a page. Every once in awhile he will dip his pen into an inkwell.

The *Writer*, a writing boy, is the third unusually rare doll automaton from Jaquet Droz, found at the Historical Museum of Neuchatel.

In connection with these, one should also mention the famous flute player from Jaques de Vaucanson (1738 to 1782) and also the mechanical duck. The flute player was highly celebrated by the musically-interested population of Europe at that period. It is historically proven that even Goethe was impressed by both.

At the end of the 18th century, the interest in automata was so great that special exhibitions were organized and books appeared about this topic, in which the secrets of these automata were revealed. Rather famous for this topic was the English book written by Dr. W. Hooper, *Rational Recreations*. Included was a nearly complete technical drawing of these wonderful mechanisms. Nearly all automata functioned with help from either magnets, air pressure, water or gravitation. Even this has hardly changed at all in the 20th century. What the automata had missing

Les automates Jaquet Droz à neuchatel

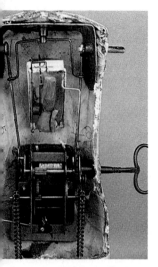

A wind-up mechanism of a walking doll made by Fleischmann & Bloedel. Both chains move the wheels in the soles of the feet.

Shoe soles with inserted wheels, propelled by two chains located inside the body (see above).

at the end of the 18th and at the beginning of the 19th century was a certain simplicity, which was required for producing larger amounts. The enormous popularity among the public caused the demand for simple automata to increase, because people wanted to buy them, not alone see them. Therefore, within a short period of time a growing industry for musical boxes was located around Geneva. The French, however, showed more interest. In Paris large numbers of new patents were granted for doll automata.

One of the most ingenious inventors was a man named Alexandre Nicholas Théroude. On January 9, 1848, he had his first doll registered, an acrobat with a spinning plate on top of the nose. Théroude was already known for his production of mechanical animals such as a rabbit which, while walking, let candy fall and a hen that could lay a golden egg. At the Paris Exhibition of 1855, he presented a goat, which moved in the same way as that of a real one. Thereafter, he specialized completely in the production of walking dolls. In 1853, he received a patent for a doll that could move forward on three wheels. In February 1854, he received another for a doll that could say "cuckoo," move its arms and close its eyes. His most famous patent was patented on July 20, 1852, for a doll that could speak three words: "Mama," "Papa" and "cuckoo." In fact, this invention was nothing extraordinary since the first speaking doll had been patented in 1824. What made this doll from Théroude so special was its simplicity, thus enabling it to be produced in large quantities. Nearly all these new productions had their first appearance at toy exhibitions, which at that time were organized in large cities of the world and which were visited by thousands of interested people. At such exhibitions, the most beautiful toys received medals and certificates, often leading to bitter competition. Patents only gave their owners a limited amount of protection, since the most successful products were immediately copied by other toy makers in a very short period of time with only slight variations. That is why one needed not only technical inventiveness, but had to have commercial talent to remain and be successful in the market.

Théroude had no such commercial talent. He always made the mistake of making too many precise technical drawings of his inventions so that his competitors had no real problem in copying his products. This is the reason why Théroude, who in 1855 was still celebrating his triumphs at the Paris Toy Fair where, among other things, he had won a silver medal, slowly but surely played no further role on the market. His company still existed until approximately 1895, when others who had been in business longer, eased him from the market.

One of those "others" was Jules Nicholas Steiner, a Parisian watchmaker, who, in 1855, began to busy himself with the production of mechanical dolls. It was not extraordinary that a watchmaker concerned himself with this topic, since the technical side of the automata was mainly based on the same principle as that of clocks. On the September 17, 1855, Steiner applied for a patent for a mechanical doll, an invention, which was very similar to that of Théroude's from 1852. It could speak, walk and had a mechanism which was very similar in design of that of Théroude's. The only difference was the fact that it could be wound-up by a key located at the hip, whereas that of Théroude's needed two pieces of string. This patent describes the mechanism of a doll which could move its head, lips, arms and legs and, when laid down, would scream. The technical drawing shows the inner mechanism, but not the joints. From 1855 onwards, nearly all dolls had fixed heads. Only the automata had movable heads. It is quite possible that Steiner, like his colleague, Cruchet, invented this clockwork mechanism. There is doubt that this doll was ever produced since no such example can be found in any collection.

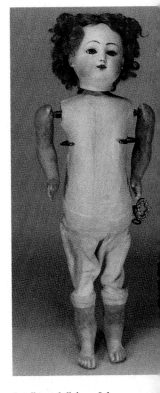

A talking doll from Jules Nicholas Steiner, Paris, circa 1878. Fine bisque head, blue glass eyes, open mouth with upper and lower teeth. When the mechanism is wound up, the head, arms and feet begin to move and the doll starts to say "Mama," "Papa."

In 1860, Steiner was mentioned in the annual trade books as a producer of toys and in 1862, he again registered a patent for a mechanical doll which he called the "Automatic Speaking" bébé. A spring mechanism moved the arms, legs, mouth and head, while a type of voice box was emitting squeaking noises when the bébé was laid down. The drawing of this patent shows the shape of the bébé with far more accuracy than the patent of 1855. The neck portion is shown very clearly and the legs correspond to that of a bébé, which we know under the name of *Bébé Gigoteur* (kicking baby). Steiner now called himself "producer of mechanical toys, exhibition models and music models, specialist of a new set screw system for toys with wheels." He was more a mechanic, which at that time was very modern, than a doll producer. In the year 1867,

J. STEINER PARIS

[Marking found on the mechanism of the doll]

Mechanical dolls, so-called "Walking Steiners," from Jules Nicholas Steiner, Paris; circa 1878.

Steiner registered a patent for a voice box, which was inserted into a stuffed doll body made of leather and in 1865 he advertised in the annual trade books, "Special factory for speaking dolls and Bébés, patented, SGDG, mechanical and with limbs." Steiner was now specializing in the production of mechanical dolls and Bébés, which he sold to the largest producer or dealer of that period.

In 1861, Pierre Jumeau advertised talking bébés and a mechanical bébé of Steiner's has been found which corresponds to the patent of 1862, with an original label attached from Steiner saying, "delivered on 27.6.67 to Mr. Jumeau."

In the December 15, 1863, issue of the girls' magazine *Poupée Modèle*, there was an advertisement saying that a Madame Chaffour, a toy dealer, had a "charming Bébé, which could walk and talk and was not always well-behaved and therefore would cry and move its arms and legs if one laid it down." This mechanical bébé was also available at Guillard, at the Gallery Vivienne in the House of Giroux and at the Brothers Susse — all toy dealers. It was the novelty of that period.

In 1869, Steiner concentrated on a new production, the "Velocipede." Ernest Michaux had invented the pedal in 1865, which perfected the new method of transportation, the Draisine, which was called the penny-farthing bicycle. In 1869, wood began to be replaced with iron and rubber was used for the wheels. It is not surprising that Steiner, who was inspired by this mechanism, plunged himself into this new production. Steiner kept the production departments for dolls and mechanical bébés, but he now specialized temporarily on mechanical cars with a new system (patented) for children and grown-ups (Trade Book 1869).

After 1871 Steiner moved three times and in 1873 one found him residing in the Rue d'Avron 60 near the "Nation." This was his final address. His speciality was mechanical dolls, walking dolls, talking babies, dolls and bébés with limbs.

The first real walking doll was finally invented in 1862 at a place far from the European market, the United States. On July 7, 1862, a certain Enoch Rice Morrison patented a product which consisted of a doll's head and a hidden clockwork mechanism in a body, and which could take small steps with its metal feet. Interestingly, this invention was patented also in England by a technical drawer by the name of A. V. Newton. A very good drawing of this doll and mechanism still exists. Most of these are girls. They are made from composition, bisque or wax, but there are also very rare ones such as *Zouaven*, *Empress Eugenie* and *Napoleon III*. These dolls were called Autoperipatetikos (Greek for to go by oneself). In December of that year, it was also protected by law in Europe. If one looks at the large number which are still in existence, quite often found with the original carton, one can assume that a great number of these were produced. Very unusual about the Autoperipatetikoes" was the fact that they could walk without getting any assistance (see page 38), which was not always the case with other dolls produced at that time. After several successful years of this Autoperipatetikos, a new product appeared on the market in 1868. It was also invented by an American, William Goodwin. A Christmas catalog of that year describes this new product as follows: "This ingenious automatic doll — presented for the first time — is a walking doll, which is pushing a cart through a room. The doll is very light and graceful and its well-built limbs and feet move very naturally. The mechanism is located in the cart and is wound-up with the help of the wheels, so that it makes a key unnecessary." The doll had a composition head produced by George Hawkins, also an American, and was brought onto the market by the largest toy dealer of New York, Althof, Bergmann and Associates. Two years later Goodwin developed another doll automaton, a girl sitting on a tricycle. This model was also so successful that other toy producers copied it.

Many companies who were attracted by the success of walking dolls started to occupy themselves with the production of this type of toy. One of these was the company Fleischmann & Bloedel which, in 1895, brought out a walking doll, whose bisque head was supplied by Simon & Halbig. A very sturdy mechanism was stored in its body, of the clockwork type, which was wound up on the side and had double chains, which ran through the stiff legs (legs were made in one piece) and thereby setting the wheels located in the soles of the feet into motion. The head and arms could also move. Furthermore, the doll could make a sound, activated by a pair of bellows also built into the body. Located at the side was a locking device. Thus, the market was revived and enriched by a large number of new products.

After winding up the mechanism, the "Walking Steiner" starts to move forward and raises its arms up and down. The wheels are located at the base, by which the doll moves.

The wind-up mechanism of the swimming doll *Ondine* enables the doll to move her arms and legs naturally. The body is made of cork, arms and legs of very light wood, hands are of metal and the head is made of celluloid. The doll can really swim.

The Bébé Téteur from Bru (described in the text) can drink from a baby bottle and has a bisque head and jointed body; circa 1890.

In 1871, the first crawling doll appeared; in 1872, the first dancing doll pair and, in 1876, even a doll that could swim, the famous *Ondine*, invented by M. Martin (see top photograph on page 32). During this period the names of doll makers were mentioned for the first time, who later became famous throughout the world. Steiner, one of the inventors of the walking doll, has already been mentioned.

Worth mentioning is the name of Leon Casimir Bru. Although this doll maker was especially well-known for his superb bébés (dolls which depicted girls between the ages of eight and 12), his automata were also very remarkable. Compared to most other doll producers who occupied themselves with moving bodies, Bru directed his attention mainly to the imitation of other important body functions like eating, drinking, sleeping and breathing. After he had received his patent in 1872 for a doll with two faces and a built-in musical box, his most sensational invention appeared in 1882 for a girl called *Bébé Téteur* which could drink a bottle of milk dry. The secret of this procedure was that a butterfly screw with a metal bow was attached to the back of the head of the baby. If one turned the screw, the metal bow would press together a built-in rubber container in the head. If one placed a milk bottle into the mouth of the baby and loosened the pressure by unwinding the screw, the milk would then be sucked into the mouth. By placing the pressure on the rubber container, the milk would flow back into the bottle. In 1892, Paul Eugene Girard designed a doll which could speak, sleep and breathe and, in 1895, the famous *Bébé Baiser* was brought out, a doll that could blow kisses. It was copied quite often later. This model, with better equipment, was produced later in large quantities by Steiner and, after 1900, by Société Francais de la Fabrication des Bébés et Jouets, (S.F.B.J.), a company which was a conglomerate of many French toy manufacturers who came together in 1899, in large quantities (see page 40).

A Parisian company, Roullet & Decamps, took a special place among the producers of automata. This company was founded in 1865 by Jean Roullet and later on was taken over by his son-in-law, Ernst Decamps. The company mainly specialized in the production of mechanical and walking dolls, producing only the mechanisms and ordering the heads, limbs and clothing from other companies. Only the assembly of the various parts was done by Roullet & Decamps. The quality of the products of this company was so excellent that firms like Jumeau in France or Simon & Halbig in Germany, who were also interested in selling automata commercially, left the production of the mechanisms completely in the hands of Roullet & Decamps. That is why one will frequently find the markings of Jumeau or Simon & Halbig in combination with "R.D.," the markings of Roullet & Decamps on automata.

In 1867, Roullet & Decamps won a prize at the Paris Exhibition for the first time. It was only a bronze medal. In 1878, in the same year that Jumeau won his first gold medal, Roullet & Decamps won a silver medal. It may be due to this event that both companies began to work together. In every respect, the products of both Parisian toy makers were a highlight in the production of automata. The dolls, with their porcelain heads of Jumeau standard, were made of bisque, had the close appearance of skin and were dressed in silk and satin.

During the association between both Jumeau and Roullet & Decamps, one of the most beautiful and well-known of doll automata was created; *Le Fumeur* (the smoker), with a rather elegant Jumeau head. As soon as the clockwork mechanism, consisting of rods, cogs, wheels and a bellows located inside the body (see right), was set into motion, the smoker would raise its right arm with the burning cigarette to its mouth and suck in the smoke via a hidden tube located in the arm. Then the smoker lowers its right arm with the cigarette and starts to raise the left arm holding the lorgnette (a pair of opera glasses) towards its eyes. It then lowers this arm and exhales the smoke, which happens when the bellows inside the body is automatically depressed. So the smoker, due to its crafty technique, can actually smoke, lift its head up and down and play a melody from a built-in music box located in the base. After 1911, the "Smoker" was offered in the Decamps' catalog in three versions, similar to those offered in the old catalogs, as follows:

— 24¾in (63cm) Smoker, a Mexican, dressed in a very rich satin costume.
— 24¾in (63cm) Smoker, Page boy, dressed in a very rich satin costume.
— 23⅝in (60cm) Smoker, a Count (Marquis Fumeur), dressed in a very rich satin costume, movable head and right arm holding the cigarette, standing on a pedestal with a music box.

DÉPOSÉ
E 9 J

[Neck markings of Emile Jumeau, circa 1880]

JUMEAU
MEDAILLE D'OR
PARIS

[Body marking from circa 1880]

Le Fumeur (the Smoker), a doll with a fine bisque head from Jumeau and a mechanism from Roullet & Decamps, which, as described in the text, can actually smoke. Marked: "Déposé Tete Jumeau Nr.5" (with tick), circa 1888.

33

On the soles of the shoes are the wheels and patent markings of a walking doll from S.F.B.J., which is illustrated on page 39 with the original box.

Another rather pretty object, which was created in 1880 during this joint venture, was a walking nursemaid with a baby carriage. The girl nurse and the baby in the carriage are both well dressed and the whole thing moves in a natural and graceful way. The most amusing thing about this is the way the mechanism is stored. Normally, the mechanism was either built into the carriage, whereby it was rather bulky, or it was hidden under the wide skirt of the nursemaid, which happened to make the nurse look rather corpulent and unshapely. Decamps, however, managed to build the mechanism so small and compact that it could fit in below the waist of the nurse, whereby the natural shape of the body was not altered. He was also able to make the mechanism so silent that one believed a real girl was walking. The only regrettable thing was the fact that the appearance of the child in the carriage was not completely perfect. It had a very unnatural posture and was in comparison too small. It also had a face of a grown-up.

At the end of 1890, the joint venture between both companies dissolved. Ernst Decamps had, at this point in time, received for the first time patents for two dolls, one of which he called *L'intrépide Bébé* (courageous girl) which could walk without the aid of a mechanism. This invention became a great success and the doll was produced up until 1921. Rather noticeable was the fact that during the period from 1900 till 1910, as most French producers were giving up their production due to the growing competition from German producers, the firm of Roullet & Decamps was experiencing a prime period. The company was being smothered with prizes, even though the reputation of the company was not entirely the same after the death of Ernst Decamps. It existed until 1972. The end of the joint venture with Roullet & Decamps meant that Jumeau must find some other toy specialist to do the mechanics so that the production of his automata was not stopped. Jumeau's new partner was a small company owned by Leopold Lambert, who presumably was related to the widow Lafosse, who managed the Steiner company from 1893 onwards. Although Lambert's products were not inferior to those of Roullet & Decamps in originality and creativity, they did, however, have distinct errors. Lambert was not able to hide the mechanism. Most of the time it was hidden in a satin covered box on top of which the doll stood. Also, the movements of the dolls differ between those of Lambert and Roullet & Decamps. Roullet & Decamps was famous for the natural movements. Lambert tried to copy these movements, but ended up with rather clownish movement. A very good example of this was the famous "Crying girl with a puppet."

A girl raises her arm up and pulls a punchinello doll up by its strings so that it can also stand. It lowers its head, looks down at the doll, lowers its arm, whereby the doll collapses into a heap and turns away so that it can wipe away a glass tear with a lace handkerchief from its cheek. To increase this effect, a melody from the opera "Carmen" starts to play when the doll is set into motion.

A doll with far less extravagance is found in an English collection and it has the unmistakable facial characteristics and clothing of a Jumeau doll. It is trying to catch a butterfly attached to a limp spring, with a small net held in her right hand. This doll is also standing on top of an ordinary musical box, which tries to increase the effect of the movements made by the doll by playing a melody. After 1890 nearly all productions of automata have a tendency towards performance and dramatics. Music boxes with only one doll, with graceful and imposing movements, did not attract the public's attention anymore. Objects that were copied too often, for example the girl behind a baby carriage, a doll playing a violin or a normal walking doll, could not awaken the interest of customers and, therefore, they slowly disappeared from the market. They were then replaced by so-called "Tableaus vivant" (living elements) in complete scenes such as two children playing in a garden, seven girls dancing ring-around-a-rosy or even a group around a coffee table with a bizarre center of attraction, a dog playing a fiddle. So strong was the appeal and pleasure for things that moved, that even a normal toy doll had a built-in mechanism, such as, for example, moving eyes described in many various patents.

In the middle of the 19th century, sleep eyes were already in fashion. In 1882, the Bru company invented a doll called the *Sleeper* which had eyelids that closed over the eyeballs. At approximately the same time, Steiner produced a doll with a lever mechanism located behind the ear, which when moved, opened or closed the eyes.

In Germany in 1880, Heinrich Stier patented a doll with glass sleep eyes which moved with the help of lead weights. According to its position, it would either open or close its eyes. Simon & Halbig also had great success with its 1890 patent for the eyes which could move from side to side and were called "flirting eyes" and, in 1906, the company received another patent for a doll that could blink. Over a period of time, dolls with other kinds of movements enjoyed a certain amount of popularity such as dolls with moving lips, dolls that could breathe, whistling dolls, dolls that could turn their heads and crying dolls. Actually, there was nothing left that had not been tried.

A crying doll with puppet and glass tears in the eyes; the mechanism and musical box are described in the text; marked: "211;" attributed to Jumeau.

Sound holes in the chest of a *Bébé Phonographe*. (Description of the invention by Edison is in the text.) Further photographs of this doll may be found on pages 50 and 51.

DEPOSÉ
TÊTE JUMEAU
11 H4

[Neck marking of a phonograph doll from 1893]

BÉBÉ JUMEAU
Bte. S.G.D.G.
DEPOSE

[Body marking]

The talking dolls from Théroude and Steiner have already been mentioned. However, these could not speak more than three words. This all changed in 1877 when Thomas Alva Edison discovered a machine that could record and play back voices. This invention, called the phonograph, was created by accident, when he tried to record news that came over the telephone. Edison, who tried to protect everything with patents that could have been of commercial interest, understood immediately the great importance of this invention in the toy industry. That is why, in 1878, he patented a doll which was equipped with a phonographic device. Only 11 years later, in 1889, did Edison have the confidence to bring this product onto the market and in 1890, the people of New York, for the first time, were able to hear a doll speak. The dolls that were exhibited could tell tales in succession and every day huge crowds fought to get a glimpse of these technical wonders. The phonograph was hidden in the body and was activated by a winder located in the waist. The steel body was made in the United States and the head was made by Simon & Halbig. In spite of this revolutionary invention and the first initial interest of the public, the phonographic dolls were commercially a flop. The main reason was its price, $20, which at that time was too expensive. All efforts to try and boost the sales of this doll did not have positive results, especially when Edison noted that even with his patents, other competitors were copying and reproducing his dolls.

The most well-known of these was the *Bébé Phonographe* made by Jumeau (see page 50), which was produced for the first time in 1893. It could speak and sing and had a vocabulary of up to approximately 75 words. In addition, when one bought this doll, one also received extra cylinders on which texts in various languages such as English, French or Spanish were recorded. Jumeau's "foreign language record" was later surpassed by an Italian doll maker, Guglielmo Voccia, who invented a doll, called *Lily* which could speak nine different languages "fluently." Jumeau's *Bébé Phonographe*, with a socket head made of a very fine bisque, carried its mechanism in an original Jumeau composition joint body. The mechanism was covered with a metal lid. The interchangeable wax reels located in the breast of the doll were started or stopped by a locking device situated on the back of the doll. Jumeau soon discovered that this doll was not commercially successful. The appeal of this doll with its limited number of languages quickly lost the children's interest. In addition, its high price caused the sales of this doll to drop rather rapidly after only a few years. In 1899, Jumeau stopped this production. Several other manufacturers, however, tried to use this invention commercially. They soon discovered that they did not have the public interest either and they stopped their production as well.

A new climax was reached around 1900, as musical boxes combined with moving figures were produced. The improved technical capacity, for example, the music boxes, could now store six or more melodies and due to the hard competition, the prices dropped. Favorites were the dolls that played musical instruments as well. Between 1901 and 1902, a French toy manufacturer, Fernand Martin, developed a piano player that could play "God Save The King" in honor of King Edward VII's accession to the throne. Also, animals that could play, for example, a violin, sold like hotcakes. One of the many French novelties which was very popular around this period was the *Marotte* (Whimsical) or the *Schwenker* (Pivot doll) (see page 103). This was a doll's head attached to a wooden rod with a musical box. The rod had to be swiveled before the music box started to play. Soon these products were offered in various different models. A rather rare example was produced by an unknown French manufacturer which not only had a head, but also the complete body with arms, legs and feet of a doll. Another model, which at the same time could be used as an umbrella, is very rare today and, therefore, a very sought-after collectors' piece (see page 102). In France, the "swivelers" were mainly produced by Dechais, Jullien and Rabery & Delphieu, and in Germany by Franz Schmidt, Ed Kahn and Zinner.

The heyday of the automata came to an abrupt stop when World War I began. After the war, the public's interest in automata was no longer the same. Naturally, several companies like Roullet & Decamps and Vichy continued their production, but the great years of the automata had passed.

A German walking doll automaton with bicycle; bisque head; marked: "1079 Halbig S&H Germany 2;" circa 1895. By winding up the mechanism, the doll can move forward all by herself, pushing the bicycle alongside.

An early 10¼in (26cm) walking doll (so-called Autoperipatetikos); breastplate head made of glazed porcelain, cloth upper body with leather arms, trapezoidal-shaped skirt made from a cloth-covered cardboard used as the cover for the mechanism, lead feet, old dress made of silk; patent marking is found on the bottom of the doll dated "July 15, 1862" (see above). The mechanism is started up with a key located at the side, which then sets the doll into motion.

Translation of the text found on the box of the doll on the opposite page: "Very Important So that the Bébé can walk properly, it is advised to place it on a flat, but not smooth surface. Move the arms slightly forward before it starts to walk, so that it can keep its balance. Functions of the Bébé Walking doll with life-like eyes. On the right side of the Bébé there is a key located to wind-up the mechanism and on the back of the neck there is a button, which can be pushed in and out. The button when depressed stops the doll; when released starts the doll moving. It is sufficient: 1. To wind up the spring with the key, while the button is pushed in. 2. Release the button and the Bébé starts to walk, whereby the eyes move from left to right."

Walking doll with tin wagon, head made of papier-mâché, molded hair, metal body with metal hands and feet, wagon marked as below. The mechanism is located at the bottom of the wagon. It is wound up with a key located at the side. The wagon starts to move forward and pulls the doll along. The doll makes proper strides.

Markings found on the wagon:

W.M.F. GOODWIN'S
Patents
Jan. 22nd, 1867
Aug. 25th, 1868

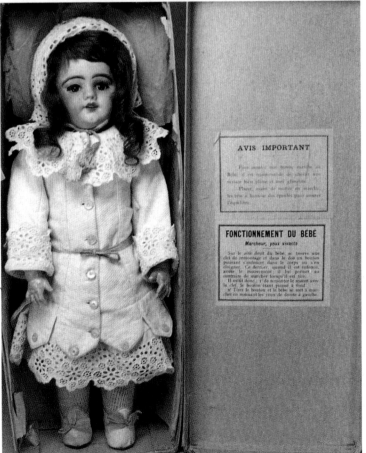

AVIS IMPORTANT

FONCTIONNEMENT DU BÉBÉ
Marcheur, yeux vivants

16⅞in (43cm) walking doll automaton, S.F.B.J., Paris; marked: "5 DEPOSÉ S.F.B.J.;" head made of bisque, blue flirting eyes, open mouth with teeth, pierced ears, light brown real hair wig, body made of wood and composition; wears a beautiful old piqué cotton dress with lace and mother-of-pearl buttons, matching bonnet, undergarments, stockings, metal shoes covered with leather; original box with instructions; original condition; circa 1905. By winding up the mechanism, the doll can start to walk without assistance; at the same time the arms move back and forth and the head and eyes move from left to right. The text from the box is found on the opposite page.

5
DEPOSÉ
S.F.B.J.

[Marking of the doll in the box]

39

A 21⅝in (55cm) walking doll that can blow kisses (half automaton) from S.F.B.J.; bisque head, blue sleep eyes, open mouth with teeth, pierced ears, original blonde mohair wig, composition body with walking mechanism; wears old dress made of silk, matching hat; circa 1900. Through the movement of the legs, the head moves from left to right and blows kisses.

An amusing tongue-showing doll automaton, bisque head from Jumeau, music box and mechanism made by Lambert of Paris; original condition, circa 1890. When the mechanism at the base of the box is wound up, the box starts to play a tune and the doll starts to move its hands towards its nose and sticks out its tongue.

"Girl with flowers and a small mirror" doll automaton from Lambert, Paris; head made by Gaultier, original condition, head and hands made of bisque, blue eyes, pink-colored silk dress with collar of lace covered with pearls; circa 1885. At the base is a music box with mechanism. When this mechanism is wound up, the doll will begin to move her head back and forth and slightly bows forward towards the flowers and the small mirror. The arms move up and down. At the same time the melody "La grosse Cuisse" starts to play.

13¾in (35cm) *Violin Player*, unmarked automaton; head made by Gaultier, original condition, a very fine bisque head, fixed brown paperweight eyes, closed mouth, body made of cardboard, metal arms and hands connected to the body by wires, attractive and elegant clothing made of silk, cloak with pearl border; circa 1880. If the mechanism is wound up, the head swings to and fro and the doll starts playing the violin with the right arm. There are three different melodies.

45

The Flower Child, French automaton, producer unknown, German bisque head, no markings, fixed blue glass eyes, open mouth with teeth, composition hands, wooden legs; original condition; 16½in (42cm), including the base 21⅝in (55cm); circa 1900. When the mechanism is wound up, the head begins to move back and forth. The right arm moves and a melody is played.

Opposite page: *Girl with Guitar*, mechanism made by Lambert, Paris, unmarked head made of fine bisque mounted on a breastplate, fixed blue eyes, closed mouth; original condition; with base 24¾in (63cm); circa 1885. When the mechanism is wound up, the head moves back and forth, up and down. The right hand plays the guitar while the left arm lifts the guitar up and down. It makes the doll look as if she is really playing the guitar. The music box plays two different melodies: "Le Trouveie" and "La Valse Bleu."

The key to the mechanism belonging to the doll on the opposite page is marked: "LB" (Lambert, Paris).

46

A Clown with Drums, a half automaton, bisque head presumably made by Simon & Halbig, marked: "Germany 7/0," fixed blue eyes, open mouth with upper teeth, original brown mohair wig, wooden body, original clothing; original condition; 13¾in (35cm) tall and 7⅛in (18cm) long; circa 1900. By pulling the wagon, the head and arms begin to move, the right arm strikes the drums.

Covered Arch, two doll automata; Gebrüder Heubach, marked: "6" character heads made of bisque, closed mouths, painted hair, composition bodies (the upper part of the bodies, arms and heads are connected to the mechanisms with wires), turquoise and pink silk original clothing; painted bench; the arch is decorated with flowers, bows and leaves; box covered with colored paper; circa 1900. If the handle is turned, both dolls begin to move and bow their heads forward, while a melody is played.

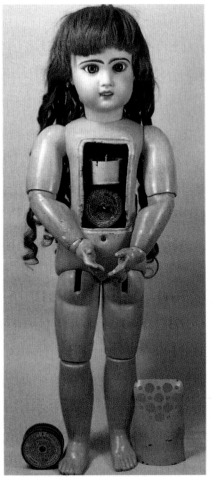

V 11

[Neck marking]

BÉBÉ JUMEAU
Diplôme d'Honneur
BREVETE S.G.D.G.

[Body marking]

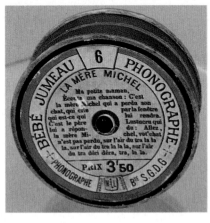

50

26¾in (68cm) Jumeau *Bébé Phonographe*; neck marked: "V11," body marked: "Bébé Jumeau Diplome d'Honneur BREVETE S.G.D.G.;" socket head made of very light fine bisque, open mouth with six upper teeth, original real hair wig, composition body with ten joints, mechanism built in chest with a metal covering with holes, very beautiful old dress made of cotton, richly decorated with lace and pleats, original shoes and stockings; circa 1895. Once the wax reel is placed inside the chest and the mechanism is wound up, the doll starts to sing the song "La Mere Michel."

The mechanism key from *The Smoker* is marked: "LB" (Lambert, Paris).

The Smoker, an automaton made by Lambert, Paris; bisque head made by Jumeau, open mouth with teeth, hands and legs carved of wood, beautiful old clothing, music box and mechanism in the wooden base; circa 1890. In the right hand the doll is holding a cigarette in a cigarette holder. When the mechanism is wound up and the cigarette is lit, the doll moves its right hand towards the mouth and takes a puff from the cigarette and then exhales. The right arm moves up and down and the head from side to side. At the same time a melody is played.

Opposite page: *The Dancing School*, automata made by Lambert, Paris; bisque head made by Jumeau; circa 1885. The mechanism and the music box are located in the base. When the mechanism is wound up, the large doll turns her head from side to side and at the same time moves her left arm with the glasses towards her eyes. The right arm with the baton moves up and down as if she is conducting. The smaller doll spins around while the music is playing. The large doll is 17¾in (45cm), the small doll 7⅛in (18cm). *From the Carin Lossnit Doll Museum.*

German Dolls

Biedermeier doll; shoulder head made of glazed porcelain, molded black painted hair, blue painted eyes.

Even though porcelain was invented over thousands of years ago in China, the art of porcelain manufacturing was unknown for several centuries in Germany. Only in 1790 did Friederich Berger invent hard porcelain for the second time around. The first doll heads made of porcelain were produced around the beginning of the 19th century. It was the manufacturers like Meissen, Hutschenreuter and Nymphenburg who produced them. Around 1850, the doll industry began to use this wonderful material and, after several first attempts, managed in a very short time to produce its own doll heads that were, in fact, works of art and of very good quality. Below is a short summary about the development of dolls' heads and about the materials they were made of.

China, a white glazed porcelain, named after the country of origin. The doll heads came with molded hair, after being fired only once. Eyes, mouth, cheeks and the color of the hair (mainly black) were painted on by hand using natural paints and, after being glazed, fired for the second time.

Parian, a white unglazed porcelain, was invented around 1850. This material is very similar in appearance to that of Parian marble, after which it is named. The eyes, mouth, cheeks and molded hair (mainly blonde) of these doll heads were hand-painted. The Parian head was only fired once. In some rare cases, one will be able to find glass eyes and some dolls with wigs.

Bisque, an unglazed porcelain, was popular by 1860. Doll heads made of bisque were only fired once before the painting was done. This was then followed by the application of the skin color, cheeks, mouth, eyebrows and eyelashes which were then painted and the head was fired for the second time. Molded hair was replaced with the more popular wigs. These dolls had mainly glass eyes.

15¾in (40cm) Kestner; marked: "XI," bisque socket head, brown sleep eyes, closed mouth, composition body with eight joints; circa 1885. This doll seems to have been cast from the same mold as the doll on the opposite page.

Opposite page: A very lovely 19¼in (49cm) Kestner doll; fine bisque head, marked: "13," blue glass eyes with paperweight effect, real hair wig; circa 1890.

As mentioned before, many doll collectors and doll lovers today overlook those dolls that have molded hair and that is why they are not properly valued. The reason for this may be found in the fact that these dolls were produced in large quantities and are rather simple. However, there are a lot of models from that period between 1860 and 1890 that show a high standard of quality and are proof of true masterpieces of the art of molding. Not all dolls are marked because the English trademark laws only appeared August 23, 1887, and then followed the International Export laws in 1890, dictating that all goods shipped to England or any other foreign countries should be identified by a marking from the land of origin. That is why after 1890 you will quite often find, independent from the markings of the company, a marking with the addition "Made in Germany." Companies often had more than one marking. On the following pages are several markings which are assigned to the dolls shown.

Heads and Bodies

The earlier heads consisted of a neck and breastplate in one piece. If the shoulders were molded-on, then they were called shoulder heads. Around 1870, however, there were rare cases where a socket head was mounted on a breastplate. From approximately 1880 onwards, the socket heads dominated. In the beginning, the bodies consisted of cloth and leather while the forearms and sometimes the lower legs as well were made of porcelain. After 1880, jointed bodies were mainly used, made either out of wood or composition. The porcelain heads produced around the beginning of the 19th century were rather simply modeled and painted. Also, the porcelain had such a strong gloss that the heads did not appear real enough to find any interesting buyers. Therefore, the change was made to the Parian material, which had been invented around 1850, for the production of dolls' heads since it had a rather natural appearance. Because this material was unglazed, it did not shine as strongly and, therefore, had an agreeable matte appearance.

There are Parian heads that are extremely beautiful, since their heads, hairdos and faces had been well molded and painted. It is a great pity that these were only produced for a short number of years because around 1870, they were pushed to the side by their wonderful and charming sisters, whose heads were made of bisque which were beautiful and perfect. Bisque has until recent times remained the most important material for the production of dolls heads. A further improvement has not taken place, because it had been already perfected so well back in 1880. It is a fact that the most beautiful doll heads were produced between around 1870 and 1900 and that only character dolls, which were created around 1910, could compete against them.

The heyday of porcelain, Parian and bisque doll heads with molded hair, as well, did not last too long, but it was worthwhile calling attention to their existence, especially those with beautiful hairdos, which were molded with such perfection and are an example of the various hair fashions of that time. There were, for example, hairdos with middle or side partings, several different partings and without; short curls or long, corkscrew curls or waves; there were plaits artfully made with all kinds of curls piled or intertwined, decorated with bows and ribbons, flowers, clasps, combs, jewelry, medals, hair nets, with or without pearls. Also included were whole tops of blouses with lace and frills, as well as headgear such as peaked caps, bonnets, hats, military head wear and many other interesting things wonderfully molded by hand. Also, the many different kinds of doll faces, whether ladies' or sweet children's faces still charm collectors today. However, all the beauty and perfection of these dolls' heads with molded hair does not change the fact that they were soon out of fashion. Even so, they are produced right up to today in small numbers and more often or not are the simpler versions. Around 1880, doll makers brought onto the market dolls with the most lovable and idealistic faces made of bisque and, as a novelty, with wonderful wigs made of silky real hair, whose natural effect could not to be beaten. All the children wanted to own these lovely dolls so that they could create their own hairdos. They did not care if the fine hair was a mess and that these doll children looked like "Struwelpeter" (Scruffy Peter).

On pages 74 to 85, a series of very significant and beautiful early Kestner dolls are introduced. These were produced between 1880 and 1890. Around 1890, the doll industry also took over this development, which made these new techniques possible. The dolls received sleep eyes, open mouths with teeth and many other features, which was in fact an advancement, but in some cases it gave the doll a stupid expression. Many new changes were introduced, but the quality of the dolls had dropped noticeably. These dolls were already being produced in large numbers for sale at home and abroad at rather reasonable prices. Many children all over the world have played with them because, as a general rule, they were, in fact, toys and were not only meant to stand behind glass, which was more often the case with the more expensive dolls. However, today collectors are very happy if by great chance these wonderful and valuable dolls that once stood behind glass have been found to have survived all those years.

[Neck marking from a doll made by Simon & Halbig, circa 1882]

A doll from Kling & Co. with a molded upper part (more description on page 63).

Neck marking of a character doll from Gebrüder Heubach, circa 1910.

23¾in (58cm) Kestner; marked: "128," a very beautiful piece in original condition, socket head on a very lovely molded shoulder plate (both made of bisque), original wig on a plaster dome, cloth body, forearms made of bisque, original clothing; circa 1885.

F. made in 10
Germany
243
J. D. K.

[Neck marking from a Kestner, circa 1912]

Manufacturers

Before 1900, there were a great number of manufacturers in Germany which had produced porcelain doll heads. However, only a few of these had their own porcelain factories. The other doll manufacturers (one should understand what is meant by the word factory, since here it is meant differently, because most of these were very small family businesses) produced, for example, leather, cloth and hollow bodies, arms and legs made of composition, wigs, dolls' eyes, undergarments for dolls and clothes, hats, suitcases, shoes and many other accessories. The porcelain heads, as well as other parts, were supplied by the porcelain factories who, while producing for themselves, acted also as suppliers.

Three large companies with their own porcelain factories dominated the industry before 1900. These three doll manufacturers that every doll collector should know and every doll lover should remember are Johann Daniel Kestner, Jr., Simon & Halbig and naturally, Armand Marseille.

For the period after 1900, the companies Kämmer & Reinhardt (did not have its own porcelain factory) and Gebrüder Heubach are worth mentioning. One can argue about whether one should honor either Simon & Halbig or Kestner as being the most important German doll producer. It is a fact that both companies, besides producing simpler dolls' heads, produced the most first-class doll heads ever to be created in Germany. If one should find such a first-class doll without any markings, one can assume it was probably made by one of these two companies because, as a rule, smaller companies were unable to set such a high standard of quality. This may be attributed to the fact that only the larger doll factories were able to provide the necessary skilled workers, as well as the necessary equipment to produce such first-class dolls. Naturally, other German manufacturers produced excellent dolls, such as Armand Marseille (who specialized in producing good average quality), C. F. Kling, Bähr & Pröschild, Alt, Beck & Gottschalck, only to mention a few, but the size of the production, variety, beauty and quality could not surpass that of Kestner or of Simon & Halbig. Below is a short biography of several manufacturers.

Johann Daniel Kestner, Porcelain Factory, Waltershausen

One can say that Kestner, between 1870 and 1890, produced the largest selection of German dolls with bisque heads. That is why he called himself the "King of Dollmakers" and chose a crown as his trademark. We can only give him this title for Germany because in France, it was Jumeau which had taken the title of "Roi des Poupées." It was around 1870 when the grandson, Johann Daniel Kestner, and a few close colleagues of the company led the company to its greatest fame. His grandfather had founded the company in 1805 and had worked his way up in the business world. In 1860, he had bought a porcelain factory. In 1872, his grandson took over and he continued the company's tradition as well as expanding it. Before 1900, Kestner was one of the few doll producers in Germany that produced his dolls fully dressed. He not only produced dolls' heads for his own use, but exported these as well as the fully-dressed dolls to many other countries in the world, especially the United States, but also to France. The most exquisite dolls were produced before 1900. Afterwards the quality of the dolls dropped drastically and only after 1908 were the top dolls like the character dolls (see page 94) and the exotic dolls produced again.

Simon & Halbig, Doll and Porcelain Factories

In 1870, the companies Simon of Hildburghausen and Halbig came together and called themselves Simon & Halbig Porcelain Factory, located in Gräfenhain near Ohrdruff, Thüringia. Complete dolls were produced in relatively small numbers. The company was more a supplier of dolls' heads and parts for many other companies in Germany, France, the United States and other foreign countries. From 1870 on, many wonderful dolls were produced, at first with molded hair, but later, from 1880 onwards, with wigs. These were mainly produced for Germany and the United States, but dolls' heads were also produced, which were often marked with "DEP" (Deponiertes Geschmacksmuster).

15¾in (40cm) Simon & Halbig;, marked: "DEP 4," light bisque, fixed dark blue paperweight eyes, pierced ears, composition body with eight joints; circa 1885.

S 10 H
949

These dolls' heads, which were adapted to the French taste, were only assembled in France with paperweight eyes, French bodies, wigs and clothing, and were then sold as French dolls. The same dolls' heads but with German glass eyes, bodies, wigs and clothing were sold in Germany, because the French model was liked very much there. Their real fame came only when the company produced the very expressive character dolls for the 100 series of Kämmer & Reinhardt around 1910. In addition, Simon & Halbig produced its own beautiful character dolls and exotics (see page 88 [below left] and page 96).

Armand Marseille, Porcelain Factory

The name Armand Marseille had nothing to do with a French company, but with a German manufacturer. In 1880, Armand Marseille, son of French immigrants, founded his own porcelain factory. His production, which started out rather small, reached tremendous proportions by 1890. One can correctly assume that he had a larger output of dolls' heads and parts than any other manufacturer at that time. Great numbers of his heads were exported, especially to the United States. He produced medium quality products, but occasionally a doll would pop up that had a very high quality. Among these were also character dolls (see page 101) and exotics. Today one has come to the conclusion that Armand Marseille did not produce his own doll bodies and, therefore, his dolls' heads can be found on a great number of different types of bodies.

Gebrüder Heubach, Doll and Porcelain Factory, Lichte, Thüringia

The company Gebrüder Heubach is especially worth mentioning. What would this world be like without its funny and audacious figures? This very old company was founded in 1800. It started out as a clay pit and, by 1830, it became a porcelain factory. However, in the beginning it only produced household crockery. Only after 1900 did it obtain its famous name in the doll industry. The company mainly produced character dolls in large variations and individuality. As a rule, they were not luxury dolls. The majority of these dolls were either funny children or curious figures (see page 106).

C. F. Kling & Co., Porcelain Factory, Ohrdruff

This company was founded around 1835. At first it mainly produced household commodities. Only in 1875 did Kling begin the production of porcelain dolls, as well as bisque doll heads, which were of medium to high standard of quality. The company was known for its exceptionally beautiful doll heads made of glazed porcelain and bisque with molded hair, flowers, jewelry, upper parts of blouses and head gear (see page 62).

Kämmer & Reinhardt, Waltershausen

After 1900, a certain stagnation occurred in the doll industry. Most people were used to all these beautiful dolls and the doll producers were looking out for new sales ideas. Since the height of the doll beauty had been reached, one naturally had to go and find other ways and means to interest the public again. The first sign of realistic dolls was seen in 1908 in Munich when Marion Kaulitz introduced her Munich Art Dolls. Kämmer & Reinhardt was founded in 1886 by the sculptor Ernst Kämmer and the salesman Franz Reinhardt in Waltershausen. They did not own their own porcelain factory, but produced mainly doll bodies. Over the years this company built up a solid reputation because it produced dolls of very high quality, especially since Simon & Halbig had taken over the production of the bisque heads. Franz Reinhardt, avant-garde artist, who had a very good nose for business, saw the big chance for realistic dolls and did not hesitate to take risks. A Berlin artist made the first designs and Simon & Halbig took over the production of these realistic dolls. That was when the famous 100 series of today was created, whose high quality and characteristic individuality could not be reached by any other company. Nearly all the larger companies at that time tried to reach this standard by creating their own designs (from which several beautiful individual models were created), but more often than not Kämmer & Reinhardt dolls were copied or changed. A similar series either in Germany or overseas was never produced.

[Neck marking of a character doll 117/A from Kämmer & Reinhardt, circa 1912]

[Body marking]

[Neck marking from a doll made by Kämmer & Reinhardt]

61

Left-hand page: 16½in (42cm) C. F. Kling & Co.; marked: "151," a very sweet girl's face, breastplate head made of light colored bisque, molded hair, molded upper part of a blouse (see page 57), fixed blue glass eyes, leather body with forearms made of bisque, old clothing; circa 1885.

Above: 16⅛in (41cm) Alt, Beck & Gottschalck, marked: "894 X 6," a very lovely doll with a blue shawl (after the Queen Louise of Prussia); circa 1880.

17⅜in (44cm) C. F. Kling, marked: "128," German doll styled in the same way as fashion dolls, head of light bisque, fixed brown eyes with paperweight effect, closed mouth, molded blonde hair with a black painted molded comb, body made of kid leather, forearms and legs made of bisque, molded and blue painted boots, beautiful dress made of gray satin silk with pink colored bands around the waist, ornamental flowers, lace trimmings, earrings and necklace made of black stones, undergarments with lace and frills; circa 1885.

15¾in (40cm) Parian doll; unmarked, shoulder head
made of Parian, molded hair, molded upper part of a
shirt, forearms made of Parian; circa 1865.

19⅝in (50cm) Parian doll; unmarked, "Empress
Eugenie" model, shoulder head of Parian, molded hair,
back of head has a molded hair net, molded upper part
of a blouse, body made of leather; circa 1865.

23⅝in (60cm) Simon & Halbig; marked: "S12H Simon & Halbig," breastplate head of bisque, molded hair, fixed brown glass eyes, leather body, old clothing; circa 1885.

24¾in (63cm) Heubach, Wallendorf (presumably); marked: "W," breastplate head made of very light bisque, molded hair and molded bonnet, painted blue eyes, leather body; circa 1890.

20⅞in (53cm) unmarked; bisque breastplate head, molded hair with molded black hair band, painted blue eyes, leather body; circa 1875.

C. F. Kling & Co.; marked: "151," light bisque breastplate head, molded hair, fixed glass eyes; circa 1885.

22¾in (58cm) Alt, Beck & Gottschalck, a so-called *Highland Mary;* marked: "1000/11," breastplate head, arms and legs made of a very light colored bisque, molded hair, fixed glass eyes with gleaming irises, feathered eyebrows, old clothing; circa 1885. A very rare and sought-after doll.

C. F. Kling & Co.; a very lovely pair of dolls, marked: "153,5" (boy) and "131,4" (girl), light bisque breastplate heads, molded hair, gray-blue glass eyes with paperweight effect; circa 1880. The 16½in (42cm) boy has a leather body. The 14½in (37cm) girl has a cloth body with forearms and legs made of bisque.

Right-hand page: 20⅞in (53cm) C. F. Kling & Co.; an especially sweet doll child, marked: "182," light bisque breastplate head, molded hair, fixed blue glass eyes, leather body, bisque forearms; circa 1880.

70

15¾in (40cm) German doll similar to a fashion doll; unmarked, a very fine bisque breastplate head, delicate painting of the eyebrows, eyelashes and mouth, apple-colored cheeks, blue glass eyes with paperweight effect, closed mouth, old blonde mohair wig, body, arms and hands made of leather, an old two-piece dress in the fashion of that period, made of striped silk with pleats and a satin bow on the skirt; circa 1875.

The following early Kestner dolls (see pages 74 to 85) are among the most beautiful and rarest German dolls that were ever produced before 1900. Not only do they have beautiful and adorable faces in common, but in general they also have very expressive molded features. The lips of these dolls are very well modeled and are not found on any other dolls produced during that period. Only after 1908 is one able to find this characteristic on other character dolls.

However, these earlier dolls are often very difficult to identify because Kestner did not begin marking its dolls until after 1910 with the mark "J.D.K. Jr." The earlier ones were only marked with either size numbers (series from 5 to 9), with letters (from A to P) or with both, later with a mold number. Further distinguishing marks are, in general, fine bisque, soft natural skin coloring, careful painting, no pierced ears and quite often one will find a roll of fat at the back of the neck. One means of identification for a real Kestner doll is the plaster dome (if available), which covers the opening on top of the head. To this day it is unknown whether any other company used this type of dome.

Above and on the opposite page: 20½in (52cm) Kestner; marked: "14," a so-called Kestner AT-type (German version), socket head made of fine bisque, head opening still covered with plaster dome, original real hair wig, open/closed mouth, 1in (3cm) indentation between the lips (no opening into the head), blue glass sleep eyes, German composition body with eight joints (fixed wrists) made by Kestner, old clothing; circa 1885.

These unusual dolls are called AT-types because (even with the different types of molding, especially of the mouth and nose), they look very similar to the French A. Thuillier dolls. Of the so-called Kestner AT-types, there were two versions available: one for the German market (shown here) with German glass eyes, wigs and bodies and a version for export purposes, especially for the French market with paperweight eyes (see the following pages).

21⅝in (55cm) Kestner; marked: "13," a so-called Kestner AT-type (French version), socket head made from a light fine colored bisque, fixed light blue paperweight eyes, very delicate painting, open/closed molded mouth, gap of about 1in (3cm) between the lips, roll of baby fat at the back of the neck, French composition body with eight joints (fixed wrists); circa 1885. There is no danger of mistaking this doll with a French AT because the mouth and nose are molded completely differently. As far as is known, no other doll has a mouth molded in this particular way.

26¾in (68cm) Kestner; marked: "X16," socket head made of fine bisque, very well done painting, fixed paperweight eyes, strongly shaped molded closed-lipped mouth, unpierced ears, roll of baby fat at back of neck, a compact composition body with eight joints (fixed wrists), old clothing; circa 1885.

The dolls that have the mark "X" reveal today certain puzzles. These are found mainly outside of Germany, sometimes with a French body and paperweight eyes, so that they could be mistaken for French dolls made by French producers, for example Schmitt & Fils. Further comparisons of these dolls have revealed that the marking "X" most likely had nothing to do with mold number or size. One suspects that the dolls marked "X" were made for export and this may not be so wrong, since all dolls show a very high standard of quality. Other earlier dolls with the same face, which came from the same master mold were at first marked as usual with a size number (see page 80) and several years later with the mold number 152 (see page 80, below left).

19⅝in (50cm) Kestner; marked: "13," socket head made of a fine soft colored bisque, a delightful child's face, very well painted, molded arched closed-lipped mouth, unpierced ears, French mohair wig, brown glass eyes, composition body with eight joints (fixed wrists), old silk clothing; circa 1885.

Kestner, marked: "152."

20½in (52cm) Kestner; marked: "14," bisque socket head, dreamy expression, very well painted, brown sleep eyes, a soft pink eye shadow, strong molded closed-lipped mouth, unpierced ears, roll of fat at back of neck, composition body made by Kestner with ten joints (wrists movable), old pink-colored silk dress; circa 1890.

23⅜in (60cm) Kestner; marked: "15," socket head made
of fine bisque, blue glass sleep eyes, very well painted,
unpierced ears, strongly molded pouting mouth, roll
of fat at back of neck, typical composition body with
eight joints (fixed wrists), old hand-embroidered
turquoise-colored silk dress; circa 1885.

Note: With character dolls it is not primarily their beauty, but their strong expression that makes them highly desirable. There are a few dolls that are rare and highly sought-after which are now thought to have been prototypes which were not mass-marketed because they were not pretty enough to appeal to the public.

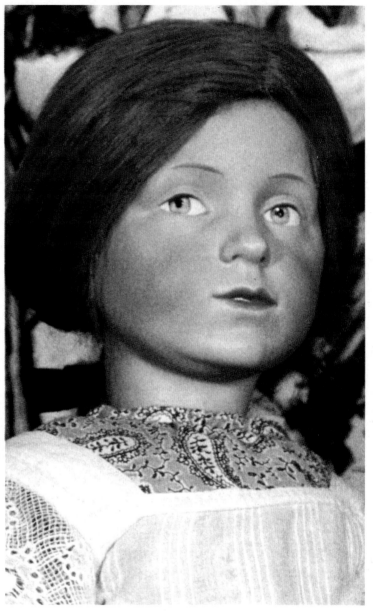

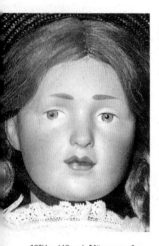

18⅞in (48cm) Kämmer & Reinhardt character doll; marked: "K (star) R 107," bisque socket head, painted blue eyes, blonde real hair wig, closed mouth, composition body with ten joints; circa 1910. According to a catalog, this doll was named *Elise*.

22¾in (58cm) Kämmer & Reinhardt very rare and realistic character doll; marked: "K (star) R 103," bisque socket head, original mohair wig, painted blue-gray eyes, closed mouth, composition body with ten joints; circa 1910.

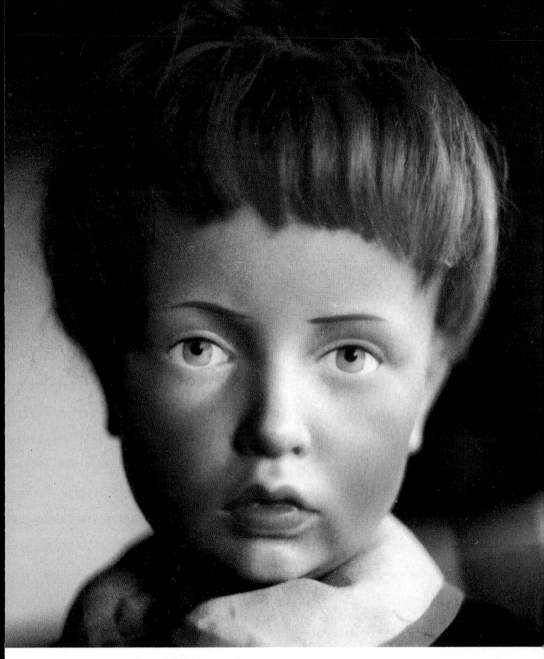

21⅝in (55cm) Kämmer & Reinhardt character doll;
marked: "K (star) R 107," bisque socket head,
painted blue eyes, closed mouth, real hair wig,
composition body with ten joints; circa 1910. According to a Kämmer & Reinhardt catalog, this doll was
named *Carlos*. *Carlos* is a doll whose face radiates
beauty and realism combined with perfection.

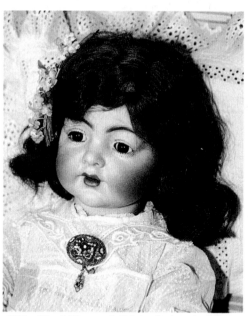

13¾in (35cm) Gebrüder Heubach character doll;
marked: "3 Germany," breastplate head, mouth with
two so-called sharks teeth, intaglio eyes, molded hair
beneath mohair wig, leather body; circa 1915.

18⅞in (48cm) Kämmer & Reinhardt character baby;
marked: "K (star) R 128," bisque socket head, open
mouth, composition body with four joints; circa 1915.

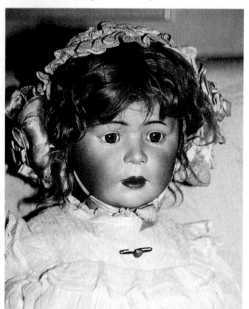

31½in (80cm) Simon & Halbig character doll; marked:
"1488 Simon & Halbig," bisque socket head, open/
closed mouth, blue glass sleep eyes, original real hair
wig, composition body with ten joints; circa 1915.

18⅞in (48cm) Kestner character doll; marked: "206,"
bisque socket head, closed mouth, original blonde real
hair wig on top of plaster dome, composition body
with ten joints; circa 1915.

16½in (42cm) Kestner lady doll called *Gibson Girl*;
especially produced for the United States; marked: "172,"
bisque breastplate head, blue glass sleep eyes, closed
mouth, original mohair wig on top of plaster dome,
leather body with forearms made of bisque; circa 1900.

Hertel, Schwab & Co. crying character doll; marked: "148 6'" beautiful bisque head, fixed blue glass eyes, open/closed mouth, original blonde mohair wig, composition baby body with bent arms and legs, original clothing; circa 1915. Inside of the doll's head one will find a small gadget which is connected to a very thin tube with a small pump which can be filled with water. If pressed, small tears come out of the corners of the eyes.

148 6

[Neck marking]

11½in (29cm) Carl Bergner, Sonneberg; very rare three-faced character doll;, marked: "C.B." (inside of a circle) on the back of the breastplate, bisque socket head (with three faces) on a papier-mâché breastplate, head crown with turning knob, fixed blue glass eyes, composition arms and legs with wooden joints, a beautiful dress with lace trimmings and matching bonnet.

[Shoulder marking of the three-faced doll made by Carl Bergner]

93

Charming pair of 15¾in (40cm) Kestner character dolls; boy marked: "182," girl marked: "212," bisque socket heads, painted blue eyes, mohair wigs, composition bodies with ten joints; circa 1915.

Opposite page: Couple standing in a flower shop; 10¼in (26cm) boy marked: "400/00," bisque round head with three holes on top, wooden composition body with six joints, original clothing; circa 1880; 10¼in (26cm) girl marked: "2," round bisque head with two holes on top, papier-mâché body with four joints, painted black boots, original clothing; circa 1880.

17¼in.(44cm) Simon & Halbig Oriental; marked: "23 164 Germany," original condition, yellow-gold colored bisque socket head, longish dark brown sleep eyes, open mouth with four teeth, original artistic dark brown wig, yellow-toned composition body with ten joints; circa 1915.

Left page: Doll dressed in silk undergarments, braided belt, hair jewelry from behind (see above) with artistically styled hair, richly decorated with glass beads, pearls, cords, flowers and braids.

Right page: The same doll now dressed in a colorful kimono made of silk and sequins, red pants with gold embroidery at the edges, necklace with two large tassels, shoes painted and decorated with sequins.

These Orientals (found on pages 96 to 99) do not only have remarkably beautiful faces, but are extremely rare and in excellent original condition.

23
164
Germany

[Neck marking of the Simon & Halbig Oriental doll]

96

18½in (47cm) Simon & Halbig Burmese; marked: "1329 Germany Simon & Halbig S&H 5," yellow tinted bisque socket head, dark brown slanted glass sleep eyes, open mouth with four upper teeth, pierced ears with original earrings, artistically fashioned original mohair wig decorated with flowers, yellow tinted composition body with eight joints, very decorative original clothing: embroidered kimono with long pants with gold tassels and braids, beautiful matching hairdo, original high-soled shoes; circa 1915.

1329
Germany
SIMON & HALBIG
S & H
5

[Neck marking]

Opposite page: 19⅝in (50cm) Bruno Schmidt, Waltershausen, Oriental;, marked: "500 1 BSW (inside of heart) 4," yellow tinted bisque socket head, fixed brown glass eyes, open mouth with four teeth, artistically fashioned and richly decorated original wig, yellow tinted composition body with ten joints, beautiful original silk clothing with borders, metal buttons and tassels; circa 1915. Note: Shoes have high platform heels and the original box is decorated with Chinese ornaments.

500
1
(B S W heart)
4

[Neck marking of Bruno Schmidt Oriental]

A pair of Kestner googlies; 11½in (29cm) boy marked: "J.D.K. Jr. 221 B 6 made in Germany," 10⅝ in (27cm) girl marked: "J.D.K. Jr. 221 A 5 made in Germany." bisque socket heads, leering glass sleep eyes, melon-shaped mouth, composition body with ten joints; after 1910.

Opposite page: Two charming Armand Marseille googly girls; marked: "323 A.M.," bisque socket heads, roguish smiling closed mouths, composition bodies with eight joints; after 1910. Left: 10¼in (26cm), right: 11½in (30cm).

Above: 14⅛in (36cm) Armand Marseille, Köppelsdorf/Thüringia, brass band "De La Santé Paris;" marked: "made in Germany Armand Marseille D.R.G.M. 246/ 1 390;" bisque socket heads, sleep eyes, open mouths, all dressed in uniforms, each doll is holding its rather realistic instrument in its hands.

Left: 14⅛in (36cm) (including rod) unknown French-produced swinging pivot doll; light bisque head, fixed blue paperweight eyes, closed mouth, original blonde mohair wig with ornamental flowers, body made of papier-mâché, music box inside the body, wooden rod for spinning the doll. When swiveling the doll, a lovely melody is played, followed by a transition melody. At the same time, the little bells hanging from silk bands start to ring.

Opposite page: 25⅛in (64cm) unknown French-produced umbrella doll with lady doll head; fixed blue almond-shaped glass eyes, closed mouth, pierced ears, original blonde mohair wig, head mounted on top of an umbrella, wears hat with an ivory ring for hanging up the umbrella, metal bells at the ends of the umbrella, carved wooden handle.

Six 7⅛in (18cm) Limbach Belton-type dolls; marked with a three-leafed clover, bisque round heads with two holes on top, fixed brown glass eyes, closed mouths, Grödner Tal wooden bodies, partly standing, sitting or kneeling; original clothing; circa 1885. One doll is holding a sheet of music, one is holding a candle.

Earlier dolls wearing traditional or working costumes were well liked. Furthermore, the accessories, it did not matter from which area (for example military, different professions or the church) were produced either by the toy manufacturer or at home. Since religion was not only practiced on Sundays and church holidays, but also at other times, children received religious objects in miniature form to play with, so as to give them religious training from a young age.

Armand Marseille, left: doll in nun's habit, bisque
socket head; right: two wooden dolls in nun's
habits; in front: a doll dressed up as a child going
for Holy Communion; front: carved wooden altar
with miniature sacramental instruments. In front of
the altar is a small priest and a small bishop holding
his staff. A small baby is lying in a coffin. All dolls
are in original clothing, circa 1900. The doll itself is
not the rarity; it is the complete group with all the
accessories.

Gebrüder Heubach, three wonderful piano babies, completely made of bisque and having intaglio eyes.

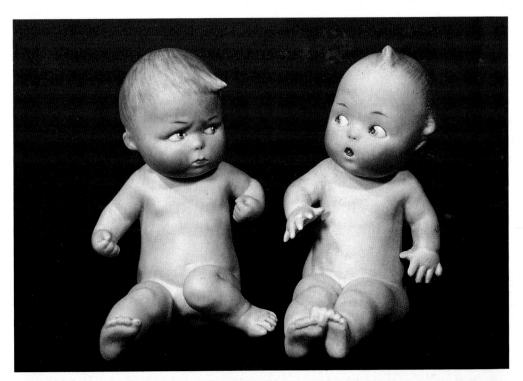

Heubach; above: two so-called position babies; below: unmarked piano baby with molded bonnet.

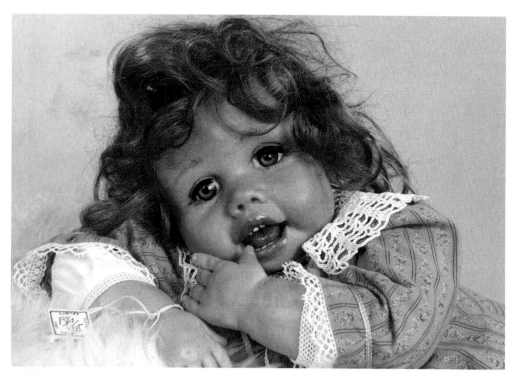

Today there are a lot of enthusiastic collectors of artist dolls made by contemporary doll makers. These doll creations are the rarities of tomorrow.

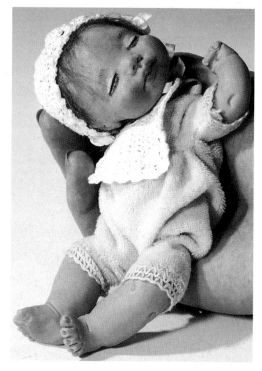

Above: A 27½in (70cm) modern artist doll by Carin Lossnitzer; charming doll child, hand molded, head, forearms and legs made of plastelline, blue glass eyes with molded tongue and upper and lower teeth, cloth body; 1986.

5⅞in (15cm) baby by Carin Lossnitzer; a cute hand-molded baby; head and limbs are made of plastelline, all parts are connected to the body using twine so that the baby is very loose-limbed; 1986.

Opposite page: A very charming 35⅜in (90cm) artist doll with a gentle smile by Rotraut Schrott; unique hand-molded piece, copied from an old photograph of a child, head, forearms and legs are made of Cernit, cloth body; 1985.

Collecting Antique Dolls

How to Collect Dolls
Practical Tips For the Doll Collector

by Carolyn Cook

For every collector, there was one doll that started the whole concept of a personal doll collection — somewhere a doll caught your attention and had a personal appeal that made you want to own it. Perhaps it was a doll from your childhood which accumulated so many happy memories that you could not part with it or another one from years ago that you long to replace. Perhaps it was a doll that you saw and appreciated for its artistic qualities and intrinsic beauty. Whatever the reason, and whatever that initial catalyst, that first doll is a clue to the most basic advice a collector can receive: collect only what has the greatest appeal to you. Do not buy a doll because it might be a good investment. Perhaps there will be a second market with other collectors, perhaps not. Do not buy a doll because it is in vogue at the moment. Like everything else, there are fads and changing tastes in the collecting world. Do not buy a doll because that is what your friends are buying. Buy a doll because you love it — and for no other reason. If you accumulate only what you love, the collection will always be a pleasure to you.

BE INFORMED — Learn as much as possible about your area of interest. Because there are so many types of dolls, you will probably need to limit the scope of your collection in some way. Perhaps you will specialize in dolls made from a certain material: porcelain, wax, vinyl or wood. Perhaps you prefer to limit yourself to dolls made during a specific period or dolls made in one country. Occasionally collectors specialize in dolls of one manufacturer or dolls themed in some way, such as ethnic dolls, nursery rhyme dolls or portrait dolls. Most of us are also limited by what our budget will allow.

After deciding what your area of collecting will be, do as much reading as possible on this aspect of dolls. New collectors have one advantage here over earlier collectors — the wealth of wonderful publications detailing the latest research on dolls and doll manufacturers. There are very few categories of collecting where excellent information is not available. In addition to reading everything accessible, take every opportunity to see doll collections, visit doll shows and check out museum collections. Every chance you have to see actual dolls and, even better, to handle them, will train your eye to spot the very best examples. The more dolls you see in original clothing, the easier it will be for you to determine what is original or appropriate clothing on the dolls you consider adding to your collection.

Talking to other collectors and to doll dealers can also be a source of useful information. Dealers often handle a much more extensive range of dolls than the average collector ever will. Most of them are very encouraging with new collectors and are glad to share information. Joining a doll club can also be a great learning opportunity. Many doll clubs are affiliated with the United Federation of Doll Clubs, Inc., a widely-respected organization of knowledgeable collectors.

There are several kinds of clues to search for when trying to identify a doll. Many dolls, especially the bisque dolls, are often marked with incised initials of the manufacturing company along with size and mold numbers, symbols, country of origin or references to trademarks (such as depose). Since the law was not passed until 1891 requiring that articles imported into the United States be marked with the country of origin, many dolls, especially ones popular before that time, may not be marked. Also, even after the import law was in effect, dolls could have been identified with stickers or tags which have been removed from the doll. Many dolls were made which were not intended for distribution in America and thus were not marked.

For incised marks, stamped information on the neck, body or feet, or raised numbers or letters on the neck or back, research in reference books such as the Colemans' *Collector's Encyclopedias of Dolls*, Jan Foulke's *Blue Books* or the Ciesliks' *German Doll Encyclopedia* can lead you to the manufacturer and approximate date of the doll.

Other clues to your dolls identity can be the "look" of the doll itself: molded hair styles, unusual eye mechanisms, nursing mechanisms, body styles and other features can be dated within a certain span and may narrow down the list of possible manufacturers. An original outfit may also be a clue to the doll's age and origin. Closely study the style of the garment and the type of fabric and the kinds of lace and trims used.

Once in awhile a doll is found with a note, letter or other written history. This can be very informative as long as you realistically consider the information given. Just because Grandma was born a hundred years ago does not mean her doll is that old. It may have been given to her when she was ten or twelve, or even as an adult!

BE INDEPENDENT — After seeing other collections and reading all you can, decide what you like best of all. Buy for your own taste. Doll collecting, like everything else, is subject to fads. Just because the bisque dolls are very popular right now does not mean you should not collect something else. Collectors in the 1930s and 1940s much preferred the chinas and Parians to bisque dolls and the prices of the time reflected that.

BE REALISTIC — Be sensible about the condition of dolls you buy. If you enjoy restoring them, buying dolls in less than pristine condition might make sense. Or if a doll is extremely rare, it is understandable to settle for less than perfect condition. Do not assume that restoration will improve a doll's value — sometimes it can detract from its desirability to other collectors. Also, having a doll restored properly can be expensive if you must hire a professional to do it, so make certain your budget allows for repairs when buying a broken or imperfect doll.

BE DELIBERATE — No matter how much fun buying "on impulse" is, all collectors should take stock of their collections from time to time and decide where the weaknesses and strengths are. Then the search can be focused for dolls which will fill gaps in the collection. Consider selling or trading duplicates to make room for new examples. It is always wise to give serious thought to what you need to balance out your collection before shopping for dolls. Then compare all the possibilities that are attainable. Knowing the available space for displaying a collection may dictate the size of dolls you look for.

BE SELECTIVE — Buy the very best example your budget will allow. The budget that you set for doll collecting may very well determine the type of dolls that you collect. The marvelous thing about this particular hobby is that there are interesting dolls in all of the categories and price ranges. It is almost always true, however, that the best examples appreciate the most in value.

Your motivation for collecting can influence how pristine a doll must be to add to your collection. For someone who enjoys giving a doll new life by cleaning, refurbishing or restoring it, the joy is in finding the treasure which needs to be saved. For the purist, only the all-original perfect specimens are acceptable. For most of us, our collections range somewhere in between the two extremes. If the budget does not allow for a rare character, perhaps an acceptable compromise would be to look for a more common mold number by the same company.

Within each category of dolls, too, there are factors which can greatly affect the cost. In the best of all worlds, most of us prefer to have dolls which are as original as possible and in fine and perfect condition. For many modern dolls this really is not too difficult, especially when buying from shops and dealers. It may be more difficult for the collector who looks for dolls at flea markets and yard sales to find choice pieces in original condition, but this method of collecting is also much less expensive. For collectible or antique dolls, finding all original dolls is more difficult and more costly than settling for a less-than-original example. The older or rarer the doll, the less likelihood one has of finding the all-original example. Then decisions must be made as to what is acceptable — period clothing or appropriate clothing? Original wig or replacement wig? If you are intending to enter your doll in competitions, then the more original and pristine the doll, the better. If the doll is being acquired solely for your own enjoyment, perhaps even the condition of the doll could vary — paint rubs or even small hairlines might be acceptable.

A 14in (36cm) German bisque with set blue eyes, a closed mouth and a human hair wig. It is marked with a small "6" and has a ball-jointed composition body with unjointed "Schmidt-type" wrists.

BE RESPONSIBLE — When you decide to purchase the doll of your dreams, there are certain responsibilities which are inherent in ownership — especially with the older dolls. Because much of the history of the doll is contained in its clothing, tags or boxes, it is important to keep such items with the doll. Occasionally, if a doll's outfit is in tatters, the owner might prefer to duplicate the dress in order to display the doll to better advantage. In such cases, no matter how decrepit, label and store the original clothing. The next owner of the doll may find these bits of the doll's provenance very important.

The correct display, storage and care of dolls is also a responsibility. This is mainly a matter of remembering that ultraviolet light, moisture and dust are enemies of a doll collection. Various materials are threatened to different degrees, but it is good to keep old dolls out of direct sunlight or away from intense display lights. Even new costumes can fade very quickly under such conditions. Moisture, too, can be a danger to composition, papier-mâché and paper dolls in collections. Care in cleaning these dolls is a matter of avoiding situations where water could damage or discolor dolls. Sometimes the steps collectors take to protect their dolls are more damaging than neglect. (A common example is putting plastic covers over composition dolls. These can trap moisture and lead to crazing or discoloring.) Wide temperature variations should also be avoided, especially with composition and wax dolls.

TYPES OF DOLLS — Although there are cross-overs, doll collectors seem to specialize in one of five main areas: antique dolls, collectible dolls, modern dolls, mass-market dolls or modern artists' dolls.

ANTIQUE DOLLS

Antique dolls are usually categorized as dolls made at least 75 years ago. These are made of many materials and, although they technically cover a huge span of time, in reality they begin with the late 18th century wooden dolls. Most collections do not have dolls that early because relatively few still exist. The first mass-produced dolls were the papier-mâché heads made in Germany at the beginning of the 19th century. Following those came the chinas, Parians and bisques which came primarily from Germany and France. England contributed wax dolls and America had some fine papier-mâché, cloth and wooden dolls on the market. Much information is available to collectors for all of these types.

COLLECTIBLE DOLLS

The collectible area of dolls between 25 and 75 years old includes the composition dolls, fabric art dolls (such as Lenci and Kruse), wooden dolls (such as Schoenhut), celluloid and other "plastic" combinations.

MODERN DOLLS

The modern dolls are the dolls which are under 25 years old. These can be either mass-marketed dolls or artists' dolls.

MASS-MARKETED DOLLS

Some collectors prefer the mass-marketed dolls which are widely available in toy and department stores — the *Barbies*®, *G.I. Joes*®, *Cabbage Patch*™ and many others.

MODERN ARTISTS' DOLLS

The modern artists' dolls are comprised of the dolls created by contemporary doll artists. This is a widely growing field. Although some artists' dolls are available to large segments of the public (such as Annette Himstedt's vinyl dolls which are distributed by Mattel and Hildegard Gunzel's vinyl dolls which are sold through the Alexander Doll Company), many artists have relatively small numbers of dolls available. Editions can be limited to a specific number of dolls or to dolls made during a specific period of time.

Buying artists' dolls can be complicated because some artists work entirely alone, some have a few helpers for dressing or accessorizing the dolls and some artists design or make a prototype and then the remainder of the dolls are made on an assembly line.

Certain artists sell designs to companies which make and distribute the dolls. A few artists work in at least two mediums. It is not unusual for artists to retain total control over their porcelain dolls but allow a commercial company to make their vinyl dolls. Obviously, in buying modern artist dolls, as in all the other categories, you should learn as much as possible about the dolls. If an artist hand-paints and hand-dresses all of her dolls, one would expect her productivity to be limited. Because of that, the prices of her dolls would be higher than most mass-produced dolls.

SOURCES — Where you look for dolls and where you buy them is as individual as your collection. The type of collection you accumulate is very personal. For people interested in antique dolls there are four main sources of dolls. The best sources for finding a wide selection of dolls are the many doll shows. A variety of doll dealers from several geographical areas will be gathered in one location. This gives the collector a wonderful opportunity to compare similar dolls, to talk to the dealers about the dolls' merits and to compare prices. This chance for comparison shopping has the same advantages for dolls that it has for other consumer goods.

Buying from a favorite dealer is also an option. When you know and trust specific dealers, it is easy to build up a relationship where they will look for the kinds of dolls you want for your collection. Dealers have a greater opportunity than most collectors to see a variety of dolls, so it always is an advantage to have them searching for the hard-to-find examples for you.

It is also possible to buy, sell and trade with other collectors or to obtain dolls from the original owners. Dealing with original owners takes a lot of diplomacy and tact, and is not a way to accumulate a huge number of dolls quickly, but often the prices are reasonable since the owners often do not care as much about making a profit as they do about finding someone who will cherish a treasured childhood toy.

For collectors of new mass-market dolls, a large choice is available in local department and toy stores. Artist dolls are sold by distributors, both in shops and by mail order. These dealers can be found at toy shows and through advertisements in doll magazines such as the **Doll Reader**®.

An 18in (46cm) Kestner with blue sleep eyes, original wig and clothing and a bent limb body. It is marked "made in//K Germany 14//J.D.K.//Z•226•Z."

Index